BULLIES...

THEY'RE IN YOUR OFFICE, TOO

Could you be one?

Dr. S. L. Young

Dedications

<u>To my mom:</u> Your strength demonstrated to and taught me to have courage and the fortitude to defend myself and not allow others to treat me as their personal trash.

<u>To those who are bullied:</u> Your struggles are temporary and shouldn't be used to validate your self-worth. Bullying is an action performed by those who are weak, jealous, or incapable of dealing with their own insecurities.

<u>Special thanks to the following for their time and generous support:</u> Ivy Boateng, Maureen Bell, Virginia Clay, Darrine Dickey, Gina Dunham, Lisa Fox, Joyce Goodson, Gary Jackson, C. Anthony Lawry, S. Keith Lewis, Preston Low, Bobbi Lineweaver, Brian Marhefsky, Rokib Masud, James T. Moore, Jr., Candy Reed, Sharon Savelli, and Edward Yeldell

Table of Contents

Foreword

Imagine working in an abusive work environment. What would you do; would you accept the abuse; would you report the mistreatment; or would you suffer in silence?

Workplace bullying is one reason that office workers (globally) are stifled, as many companies lack sufficient protective policies.

In the United States (U.S.), workplace bullying is legal in most jurisdictions, unless the bullying violates the protections offered under Title VII of the Equal Employment Opportunity Act protected by the Equal Employment Opportunity Commission (EEOC).

Many companies have anti-harassment policies; although, many of these same companies do not have policies that specifically address workplace bullying.

According to the Workplace Bullying Institute's 2021 "U.S. Workplace Bullying Survey" findings[1], 48.6 million Americans are bullied at work. Additionally, the Workplace Bullying Institute (WBI) projects that 79.3 million U.S. workers have either been bullied or witnessed bullying. This translates to approximately 30% of workers having had direct experience with being bullied.

In recent years, there's been a heightened focus and increased discussions about school bullies. These conversations typically detail the incident but fall short in a description about the impact to a bullying target's psychological, physical, and mental well-being. Furthermore, seldom do these discussions focus on the bullying that occurs beyond schools and in offices around the world.

Fortunately, there's an increased awareness about the effects of

---

[1] Workplace Bullying Institute (WBI). "2021 Workplace Bullying Survey" (2021). Online (workplacebullying.org/2021-wbi-survey), Retrieved: 10/8/23

workplace bullying. This increased knowledge about the impacts of workplace bullying has led to thirty-two states having introduced a "Healthy Workplace Bill" since 2003, based on data obtained from The Healthy Workplace Bill website (led by the National Director of the Healthy Workplace Campaign, Dr. Gary Namie[2]). Unfortunately, as of October 2023, the only U.S. state or territory that has enacted a law to protect employees (closest to the language in the Healthy Workplace Bill) is Puerto Rico, which implemented its law on August 7, 2020. This is extremely disappointing because, according to a 2022 Harvard Business Review article[3], there's ample documentation related to the organizational costs of incivility and toxicity in the workplace.

The goals of this book are to detail the many different types of bullying behaviors, illustrate the type of issues that occur in workplaces, and share lessons learned from these events.

The reason that time is an important factor in the review of a past situation is that anyone who has dealt with a bully understands that an individual's decision-making process can be impacted while under stress or duress from a bully.

Another goal of this book is to bring attention to workplace bullying incidents that often do not receive enough attention.

By detailing actual workplace bullying incidents, these events can be used as discussion points for fruitful conversations. These conversations can also lead to actions that drive changes that compel companies to create policies and the U.S. Government to enact laws to protect workers (direct and indirect) from workplace bullying.

---

[2] Healthy Workplace Bill (healthyworkplacebill.org)

[3] Harvard Business Review. "How Bullying Manifests at Work – and How to Stop It" (11/4/22). Online (hbr.org/2022/11/how-bullying-manifests-at-work-and-how-to-stop-it), Retrieved: 10/2/23

Preface

Work isn't usually the most exciting part of the day, unless you are fortunate to have a job that you love; however, the workday can become much longer if an employee is a target of harassment (otherwise known as workplace bullying.

Bullying is usually associated with schoolyard antics; although, very similar behavior can exist in the workplace too. Moreover, adults can find themselves ashamed, intimidated, or even fearful after an experience with workplace bullying, which can cause a target to react in a similar manner as a school bullying target.

The options to deal with workplace bullying can be very limited and troublesome for the bullying target, accused, and individual(s) who must investigate. These concerns can lead a bullying target to not report a bullying incident to someone who can address the issue and/or the target will continue to be bullied out of fear of worse treatment or the loss of a job if a bullying incident is revealed.

The case studies in this book are examples of workplace bullying that could happen to anyone. The purpose of documenting these real incidents is to provide accounts of different types of harassment from a bullying target's perspective. Furthermore, the case studies detail these situations and provide critical thinking questions, along with recommendations about ways similar situations can be handled.

A goal of mine in sharing these incidents is to help others who might experience similar bullying situations, and to also advise that bullying targets are not alone.

My primary goal of this book is to provide insight and guidance about workplace bullying behavior based on actual incidents to hopefully prevent or stop bullying targets from being tormented on an ongoing basis.

Work (for most) is a necessity but should not become a prison that leads to torment and sometimes torture for the affected individuals.

Companies have a responsibility to create and enforce documented policies that protect its resources (e.g., employees, consultants, other classifications).

<u>Furthermore, resources should:</u>

- Be informed and knowledgeable about workplace policies

- Be trained on the actions to take if a bully is encountered

- Understand the process to report inappropriate behavior (without a fear of retaliation)

Life is short and the time individuals spend at work is very long; therefore, individuals must address any bullying incidents as quickly as possible to protect themselves and others from needless abuse.

This book is a single step to raise national awareness about and combat this important topic of workplace bullying.

Chapter 1:

What Are Bullies?

Bullies are individuals who use their power, influence, strength, opinions, wealth, connections, intelligence, effort, etc. to discount the value of another individual's right and ability to be themselves.

Bullies use their influence in negative ways, which either makes them feel better (in a morbid way), powerful, and/or superior.

Bullies fail to realize that their behavior is more about themselves and less about their targets.

Bullies don't always start with the mindset to want to hurt their targets (emotionally or physically). There's usually an evolution from an event or events that make bullies feel a sense of satisfaction or happiness from their possession of power (oftentimes) because their target is passive in response to the bully.

If a target is passive in response to bullying, the bullying may continue or even worsen with aggression because the target is perceived as weak, unwilling, or unable to counter the attacks.

Some bullies are so aggressive that an active response to their behavior won't prevent future occurrences, because the bully experiences a certain level of satisfaction or enjoyment from the event. Nevertheless, a bullying target should not tolerate any emotional, physical, and/or mental abuse.

Individuals should take action to address, prevent, and/or report any bullying behavior as soon as possible to minimize future occurrences.

The actions and/or behaviors[4] of others cannot be controlled; however, individuals can and should always take action to protect themselves, their interests, and all their rights.

---

[4] Action(s) and/or behavior(s) are most times referred to in this book as an "activity" or "activities."

Chapter 2:

Types of Bullying Behavior

There are many different types of bullies that can be encountered because bullies use various strategies to accomplish their goals; however, bullies' objectives are similar, which are to manipulate others.

Types of bullying behavior used to achieve objectives:

- **Aggressive** – very forceful behavior that makes the target feel threatened

- **Coercive** – authority (real or perceived) to influence a certain action

- **Condescending** – an attitude of superiority over another

- **Connectional** – individuals within one's circle of influence who are used to influence another's behavior

- **Demeaning** – words, actions, and/or behaviors used to make someone feel less worthy

- **Direct Comparison** – the use of the treatment of others as a basis for an individual's argument

- **Dominant** – a strong individual presence used to dominant the behavior(s) of others

- **Embarrassing** – intentionally trying to bring negative attention to another

- **Extender** – information about an individual or subject matter that is used to advance an individual's objectives

- **Fear** – scare tactics used to obtain compliance based on a perceived threat

- **Inclusive** – an unrelated party who joins in on bullying behavior already in progress or that occurred in the past

- **Intimidating** – emotional, mental, and/or physical dominance to control an individual's thoughts or actions

- **Knowledge** – the use of information obtained and/or controlled by an individual to the detriment of another

- **Manipulative** – the use of an individual to achieve hidden objectives that meet a bully's needs

- **Passive Aggressive** – acting as if someone or something does not matter to an individual, but then responding in an appeasing manner to achieve their objective(s) while attempting to maintain relationships

- **Passive Resistance** – non-compliance in a manner that does not violate social norms, laws, or company policy

- **Physical** – the use of physical stature or muscular power

- **Positional** – the use of an individual's level in the organizational hierarchy to achieve their objectives

- **Quid Pro Quo** – exchange of something of value to achieve something else

- **Reputational** – an individual's historical record used to their advantage

- **Suggestive** – a comment made to influence another's thoughts, behaviors, and/or actions

Unrelated – information obtained and used to advance an individual's objective(s), even though there isn't a direct relationship to the target of the bullying behavior

- **Withholding (something of value)** – prevent another from being able to obtain something that is beneficial to achieve their needs

Bullies use these types of behaviors to take focus away from them and direct their shortcomings toward others.

Note: This chapter provides mechanisms to identify some of the many different types of bullying behaviors encountered in workplaces. The behavior types identified are representative of the more common types of workplace bullying and isn't an inclusive list.

Chapter 3:

Reasons Individuals Bully

Bullying occurs for many reasons; however, one reason that seldom if ever is given by a bullying target is that 'I asked to be bullied'.

Bullying is about the bully and bully's need for control.

By using aggression (physical and/or mental), a bully falsely believes that the only method that can be used to achieve the bully's objective is to attempt to control or manipulate someone.

> Note: There are many ways and methods to inspire resources to be more effective without the use of bullying tactics. Unfortunately, this topic is beyond the scope of this work but may be addressed in future books.

Reasons for bullying behavior include:

- Abuse of Power – authority used because it is available instead of using authority only as needed

- Disrespect – someone treated badly due to a feeling that an individual does not deserve better treatment

- Fun – enjoyment received due to treating someone badly

- Intimidation – power felt because someone else is fearful

- Need for Power – a belief that dominance equates to leadership

- Lack of Training – a false belief that bullying behavior is warranted or required to demonstrate authority

- Wanting Respect – an incorrect belief that bullying behavior will cause others to respect the bully

- <u>Retaliation</u> – repayment directed at someone for past actions or activities

- <u>Superiority</u> – a belief that someone isn't as good as the bully

A bully can use any of these reasons as motivation for bullying behavior. This is significant because a bully doesn't realize that the power used is mostly limited to the time of the action or the time that a bullying target is under the bully's influence.

A bully does not understand that bullying behavior does not legitimize power or incorrectly believes that the power used is "legitimate power." Moreover, a bully may incorrectly believe that "legitimate power" is granted based solely on an individual, their connections, or beliefs about their perceived power, which is absolutely and unequivocally wrong.

"Legitimate power" is derived from the position held, being a subject matter expert, or the rights granted by a higher authority, which does not require the use of bullying behavior to be effective.

The reasons bullies use to justify any behavior (to themselves) is simply a mask to hide the issues related to the bully's insecurities, lack of personal strength, and/or an incorrect understanding about leadership.

Bullies don't understand that proper and professional behavior is required to become a charismatic or inspirational leader. This is the type of leader who doesn't use fear and/or dominance as the platform for their leadership strength.

Chapter 4:

School Versus Work Bullies

"Bully" is a word that describes anyone who uses actions, words, power, influence, and/or connections to dominate, control, or intimidate another. It does not matter if the bully's actions are a one-time incident or an ongoing series of events, because the damage caused by bullies can result in emotional, physiological, psychological, or physical pain.

Generally, the word bullying is used to describe the behavior related to a school bully. School bullies' influence is often related to being called a bad name, demeaned behavior, alliances against the target, or physical attacks; however, the affect of the bullying can lead students to withdraw, act out, become depressed, and/or in worst cases commit suicide.

> Note: The increased number of student suicides (e.g., students who took their lives due to being bullied at school or online) is a reason that (in recent years) there is an increased effort to reduce the occurrence of school bullying.

Now, imagine if similar behavior occurred in the workplace. Would the impact be any less taxing?

The physical and emotional impact of workplace bullying could be the same or similar to school bullying. Now, couple bullying behavior with the necessity to obtain something to eat, take care of a family, or have somewhere to live. Then, these necessities can compound the effects of a bully's actions.

Targets of workplace bullies can feel trapped by the need to take care of themselves, others, and/or family. Therefore, a bullying target may tolerate bullying behavior that in other areas of their life wouldn't be tolerated. Moreover, once a bully realizes that the target won't fight back, a bully may become more powerful and at times become an even more aggressive bully.

School and work bullies may operate in different ways and

environments. However, bullies' bad behavioral tactics (that are focused on emotionally, mentally, and/or physically injury to others) are nearly the same.

Chapter 5:

Bully, Bad Management, or Bad Manners

Some might ask, "Is it workplace bullying?" or "Could it be bad management or just bad manners?" The answers to these questions are "yes."

The reason that these questions can be answered "yes" is that workplace bullying does not require the definition of a bully to be mutually exclusive from the definitions of bad management or an individual with bad manners.

This book defines and provides examples of workplace bullying. However, this chapter's primary focus is on the question "Could it be bad management or just bad manners?"

In terms of bullying, a bully, most times, intentionally decides to behave in a manner that intimidates, belittles, harasses, or uses any kind of unwarranted behavior.

Bad management (on the other hand) is a manager who does not have effective management skills or behaves in an inappropriate manner. The good news is that a resource who does not have management skills can usually be trained if there is willingness or a directive to change their behavior.

Conversely, bad manners are behaviors that are not intended to be harmful. For example, an individual may make a very direct comment that may be considered unprofessional, but there isn't intent to harm.

A resource with bad manners may have the skills and/or abilities to perform a job; although, there is usually a lack of recognition that their behavior is inappropriate and/or there isn't a desire to behave in a socially acceptable manner.

It is also important to note that workplace bullying can be intentional or unintentional:

- If someone's action is intentional, this means that the individual directed their behavior or action toward a target.

- If someone's action is unintentional, this means that the individual didn't purposely direct their behavior or action toward a target.

Nevertheless, a singular event (intentional or not) can still be a bullying incident.

Often, bullying is a private encounter between a bully and their target. Therefore, it can be difficult to reconcile bullying incidents. The reason for this difficulty in reconciliation is that a perception of bullying behavior isn't the same for everyone, as bullying is based on an individual perception of unwanted and inappropriate activity.

It is worth noting that a bullying target is no less of a target because unwanted and inappropriate behavior or action isn't reported.

The reason that this point is significant is that a target may be afraid to report an incident due to:
- Fear of not being able to care for a family due to job loss
- Retaliation
- Perception of weakness (e.g., lack of thick-skin)
- Other factors

These are a few reasons that laws must be enacted, company policies implemented, and remedies offered to address inappropriate action(s) and/or behaviors to ensure that every bullying target is protected.

The time is now to make changes that will protect all workers from abusive and toxic environments.

The best way to evaluate questionable behavior is to:

- Consider the context

- Determine the intent

- Allow some time to pass prior to a reevaluation

- Discuss any concern(s) with the individual directly or an uninterested party

Any of these approaches will allow an impacted individual to determine the reason(s) for the issue without necessarily placing focus on an individual accused of bullying.

Regardless of the approach used, it is best to address and document any unwanted or inappropriate action and/or behavior as soon as possible to prevent ongoing workplace bullying incidents.

Chapter 6:

Attempting to Intimidate a Youth

The first time that I encountered a bully was during my first job as a busboy. This was my first job with a regular paycheck. The job wasn't very difficult. My pay was an hourly rate plus tips from the servers. Moreover, there wasn't a defined amount given in tips each shift; therefore, I was at the mercy of each server.

One night, I bussed tables as usual. I cleared the dishes from the table and took them to the kitchen. Then, I returned to the dining room.

Shortly thereafter, the server (for the table I just bussed) quickly approached me. The server told me that I wouldn't be paid to bus tables in this server's section. My immediate reaction was, "I cannot believe that this server won't pay me! I cleaned the server's table, and the server is refusing to pay me for my work."

I was immediately taken back and thought to myself, "Wait a minute. This is my job, and the server is choosing to not pay me." Then, I thought, "Okay, I'll fix this."

After the initial shock, I quickly grabbed my bus pan and went to the dishwasher. The dishes previously cleared from the server's table were gathered and maybe a few more. Then, I took the dirty dishes back to the dining room. The dirty dishes were put back on the table, while making sure to be sloppy about it.

The server saw my actions and immediately went directly to my location. The server then used a few choice words to ask me about the reason that the dirty dishes were returned to the table.

At this point, the server was immediately told, "You made a decision to not pay me, and I decided that I wouldn't work for free." This action led to an icy stand-off, which forced the server to bus their tables for the rest of the night.

Later that night, one of the other servers who witnessed my actions pulled me aside and laughed with me about the incident. This server said that my actions took a lot of guts, as many adolescents would just accept the server's decision and not have done anything.

The server's refusal to pay me was reported to and dealt with by the restaurant's manager the next day. Also, the server was reprimanded and never again refused to pay me (or other busboys) to do my job.

Furthermore, the server (to the server's chagrin) was told by the restaurant's manager to apologize to me for the previous day's actions.

Questions

1) Was it appropriate for the server to withhold the payment of tips? Why or why not?

2) Could an age difference be a factor in the refusal to pay tips? Why or why not?

3) Was returning the dishes to the table an appropriate action? Why or why not?

4) What actions could be taken instead of returning the dishes to the table?

5) How would you handle this situation?

Lessons Learned

The return of the dishes to the table satisfied a need to react in anger to the server's refusal to pay tips that night. However, this knee-jerk reaction wasn't a mature response.

The first action in this type of situation should be to determine the reason(s) that tips wouldn't be paid. Moreover, the issue should not be discussed with the server any further; instead, the issue should be discussed with the manager-on-duty or the restaurant manager the next day.

By responding in an immature manner, the relationship was damaged, along with neither party acting properly. The server was wrong for refusing to pay the required tips and the busboy (me) was wrong for returning the dirty dishes to the table.

This type of issue should be handled differently (via a discussion about the issue(s) with management) to prevent further damage to the relationship. Also, by reacting in an immature manner, both parties engaged in an argument that neither party would win.

Bullying Behavior Types:
- Coercive
- Intimidating

Chapter 7:
Influence to Meet
Employee Perception

One of the biggest challenges is to be a supervisor while a loved one works in the same location and under your command.

In this case, my girlfriend and I worked on the same shift at a restaurant. I was the night supervisor; therefore, my responsibility was to assign special projects to employees who were not busy. The assignment of special projects was a dreaded activity for the employees and for me.

On one occasion, an employee asked, "Why is it that your girlfriend does not get any of the harder special assignments?" My response to the employee was, "Special assignments are given without any preference." I thought that this was a good response, but the more I thought about it the more I wondered if assignments (especially related to my girlfriend) were assigned fairly.

After further consideration about my discussion with this employee, the question continued to bother me. I then decided that I needed to ensure that the employees didn't think that my girlfriend received special treatment. Therefore, my girlfriend (I hope she does not read this) was given more difficult special assignments to ensure that the employees knew that there wasn't any special treatment.

This undesired "special treatment" wasn't received well by my girlfriend.

Questions

1) What should be done after an employee complains about unfair treatment (e.g., related to the girlfriend)?

2) Was anything accomplished by assigning the girlfriend more challenging assignments?

3) What might be the long-term consequences of this decision on employees? What about the impact to the girlfriend?

4) Were the employee's concerns appeased by giving the girlfriend more challenging assignments? Why or why not?

5) How would you handle this situation?

Lessons Learned

Actions (at times) will be driven by an individual's perceptions instead of the situation's reality, even if individuals do not receive special treatment or favoritism.

Leaders shouldn't buckle under pressure to meet employee perceptions instead of maintaining a direct focus on an issue, which in this case was that all employees were treated equally.

A leader's action shouldn't unnecessarily be influenced by others' perceptions. The key to leadership is an ability to make unbiased, fair, and sometimes unpopular decisions, as long as the decisions are made without questionable standards or motives.

A leader's role can be questioned; however, this challenge can be compounded if an individual's significant other is under their command. Therefore, the biggest challenges can be associated with employee perception related to favoritism and disparate treatment[5].

In this case, employees were given a "special project" during a slow period. Almost immediately, an employee questioned the fairness of the assignments. This employee's comments were directed toward an employee who was perceived to receive special treatment or favoritism, which specifically questioned whether the girlfriend was given "special projects" that were a similar challenge to other employees.

After succumbing to the employee pressure, an employee (the girlfriend) was given "special projects" that were a little (okay maybe a lot) tougher than others.

This treatment wasn't fair, but it allowed a leader to demonstrate (due

---

[5] Disparate Treatment – actions toward someone that are different from others in similar circumstances

to the increased number of expressed employee concerns) that another employee received equal or (in this case) more difficult "special projects."

The decision to give an employee more difficult "special projects" met a short-term goal of the leader to alter employee perception. However, it wasn't the right decision. The reason is that employees were allowed to influence a leader's decision instead of the decision being based on the best interest of all impacted parties, along with a concern for fairness.

For this example, the employees should be informed that decisions and "special assignments" were assigned fairly without any special treatment. Furthermore, the employees should've been informed that their concerns were noted and would be considered but wouldn't be used as the sole basis for any actions taken by the leader.

The issue with the leader's actions is that adjustments were made immediately after employees began to express concerns. Therefore, the employees observed that their expressions of unhappiness led to immediate action. Therefore, employees might believe that future decisions could be influenced by expressions of dissatisfaction.

A leader should make decisions as fairly as possible without being overly influenced by emotional reactions.

Moreover, it's important for leaders to make the best decision(s) possible without disparate treatment to alleviate any employee concerns that may or may not be justified.

Bullying Behavior Types:
- Direct Comparison
- Suggestive

Chapter 8:
Superiority Complex

I worked for a company that was about to relocate to another state. Around the same time, a colleague and I discussed the lessons learned and the successes experienced at this company prior to the location being closed.

During this conversation, I said, "I don't want to 'rest on my laurels'." Then, my colleague asked me in a condescending manner, "Do you even know the meaning of the words?" I immediately said to my colleague that I did understand the words. I then went on to say, "The expression means to sit on my behind and not advance."

My colleague quickly corrected me and said, "'Resting on one's laurels is to be happy with past accomplishments and to no longer advance."

My definition (although not entirely correct) was very close to the conversation's context.

Questions

1) Why might someone try to demean another for a term or definition that might not be completely accurate?

2) What would you do if this happened to you?

3) How could this situation have been handled?

4) What does the colleague's approach used to deal with this situation potentially convey about this individual?

Lessons Learned

The colleague could have used the "lack of accuracy" in the definition as an opportunity to convey additional knowledge. Instead, the conversation was used as an opportunity to demean someone.

The need to unnecessarily demean another is more about the individual who demeans instead of the other individual.

In this case, there was a missed opportunity to educate someone about the proper usage of an expression "resting on your laurels."

The amount of energy required to "demean" versus "uplift" someone is approximately the same. Therefore, someone's energy should be directed toward positive versus negative actions and/or behaviors.

Bullying Behavior Types:
- Condescending
- Demeaning

Chapter 9:

Subtle Guidance

After working at this company for a few years, I mastered the skills required to be successful at this job, which was evident by the performance awards received.

At an operational meeting, I received a few quarterly awards.

Immediately after the meeting, a colleague said to me, "It must be nice to be the manager's pet." This comment was troublesome. It implied that the reason I received numerous awards wasn't based on performance, but my close relationship with my manager.

Shortly thereafter, the same colleague and I started to discuss a newly created team lead position. At this point early in my career, I didn't have an interest in a supervisory position. Regardless, during our discussion, this colleague said to me, "You would make a great team lead, but just not on our team."

As someone who was new to the corporate world, this subtle guidance caused me to not apply for the team lead position on our team. The main reason that I didn't apply for the position was that I started to question whether I was ready for the team lead position.

The comment made by my colleague was subtle guidance for me to not apply for the team lead position. This guidance caused me to miss a great opportunity to become a team lead for a manager who recognized and rewarded my performance.

Furthermore, this manager was an excellent managerial and leadership mentor.

The real travesty was that my manager tried to encourage and convince me to apply for the team lead position, but I rejected my manager's encouragement numerous times.

My rejections about applying for the team lead position were partially due to self-doubt. Notwithstanding my internal questioning about my capabilities, the major reason that I didn't apply for the position was the comment that, "You would make a great team lead, but just not on our team" continued to resonate in my mind.

In this case, an opportunity for career advancement was lost due to an offhanded comment from a colleague. Furthermore, this comment was most likely made to prevent someone who was hired into the same training class, and that worked on the same team, from becoming the group's team lead.

Questions

1) Was it appropriate for the colleague to make this comment? Why or why not?

2) What would you do once the comment was made?

3) Would you say anything to counter the comment? Why or why not?

4) What lesson(s) could be learned from this type of situation?

Lessons Learned

An opportunity someone has shouldn't necessarily be influenced based on others' suggestions, because (at times) suggestions may be offered that are not in the best interest of the receiver. Therefore, the best option is to follow your dreams toward success and not be negatively impacted based on artificial limitations (direct or indirect) placed on you by others.

Bullying Behavior Types:
- Coercive
- Connectional
- Intimidating
- Passive Aggressive

Chapter 10:

Led to an Ambush

In a conversation with my operations manager, concerns were expressed about employee morale in this organization. During our conversation, my operations manager asked me to assemble a team of non-management employees to identify creative ways to improve morale.

I immediately assembled a team of talented non-management employees.

My team worked quickly to develop potential options to address the operations manager's concern about employee morale. My team was focused on the identification of creative and workable solutions because each team member would be impacted by the outcome of the team's work.

The employee-driven team was excited to be involved in the process to improve employee morale. After a few weeks, our team prepared a workable plan to deal with the organization's morale issues.

Once my team's work was completed, our operations manager was informed that my team's employee morale plan was ready for review. At this point, the operations manager communicated to me that our team would present the results at the next management meeting.

My team worked hard on this plan and was ready to share the results with the management team. However, our excitement didn't last long. The reason for the short-term excitement was that moments after the presentation began, a manager (at the head of the table opposite the first presenter) slammed a hand on the table and said, "It's never good enough, is it?!"

My team was flabbergasted by this loud outburst.

The reaction received to our presentation was surprising because the operations manager asked me to assemble a team to develop ideas to improve employee morale. However, my team didn't know a critical fact. The operations manager didn't tell the management team that our employee team was working on options to improve employee morale, too.

My team's presentation was stopped before the presentation got past the first slide. The management team then asked my team to leave the conference room. While the group was in the hallway, the management team had a lengthy discussion about the reason that my team would create a proposal to improve employee morale.

After the management team's discussion, my team was allowed to complete the presentation; however, the management team wasn't receptive to an employee-driven team's proposals to improve employee morale.

My team delivered a quality, but very uncomfortable presentation. Then, after this meeting, my team reflected on the attacks received during our presentation. My team also discussed the possibility that (for whatever reason) our team was purposely put into an uncomfortable position by the operations manager.

My team's belief had additional merit because the operations manager never told the management team that our team's presentation was created based on the operations manager's request.

Questions

1) What would you do if a presentation was abruptly and angrily stopped during the presentation's first slide?

2) What options were available (immediately after the management team attacked the presentation) prior to the material being presented?

3) Once the presentation was stopped, what should the employee team have done?

4) Should any of the employee team members have disclosed that the operations manager asked the team to develop the presentation? Why or why not?

5) What actions could be taken after the presentation?

Lessons Learned

The operations manager's reason(s) for not disclosing to the management team that an employee team was asked (by the operations manager) to develop an employee morale proposal (independent of the management team) isn't known.

The reason for the nondisclosure could be that the operations manager forgot to inform the management team about the employee team's effort, or the operations manager had a hidden agenda.

Nevertheless, if the goal was to create resentment between the employees and the management team, the goal was met. If the goal was to supplement the management team's initiative, then the matter should be handled differently. For example, the operations manager should have fully disclosed to the management team that an employee team was tasked to work on employee morale issues also.

Someone's motives won't always be known and/or understood. This is the reason that it is useful to ask questions about the goal and the intended audience prior to the start of an initiative. This will allow an initiative's effort to be targeted to meet the goal(s) and the expected needs of the intended audience.

Individuals should be prepared (as possible) for the unexpected. Furthermore, individuals should not let anyone cause a loss of focus or an emotional outburst. Individuals who prepare for the unexpected minimize the potential visceral response due to a lack of preparation.

Bullying Behavior Types:

- Coercive
- Knowledge
- Manipulative
- Positional
- Withholding

Chapter 11:
A Word Can
Make a Difference

Organizational work improvement activities take a lot of time, effort, coordination, feedback, and interpersonal relationship management to be successful.

For this initiative, in a new organization, I spent a significant amount of time to learn the organization, interview the leadership team to understand their needs, and also document the issues that led to the need for change.

After the information gathering activities were completed, the results were reviewed with the management team to ensure agreement or not with the direction of the findings and recommendations. Then, during the meeting, the management team approved the direction.

The next phase was to introduce the initiative to select employees to obtain their input on the organizational changes needed for improvement. Once completed, the final phase was to introduce the changes to the entire organization.

A short time later, a meeting was scheduled with the entire organization to review the new initiative to drive project management processes and organizational efficiency. Fortunately, the meeting was successful.

The goal of this initiative was to teach project managers about formal project management methodology and organizational terminology in a fun way. Therefore, during the initiative's kick-off meeting, a term that reflected a desirable behavior or a project management concept was reviewed.

Prior to the kick-off meeting, each manager was asked to identify an employee who demonstrated the desired behavior that would be highlighted during the meeting.

Once a list of candidates was created, the operations director selected an individual to be recognized. Then, during the kick-off meeting, an employee who demonstrated the desired skill and/or behavior was recognized and was also given a certificate, along with a small bonus.

After the meeting, there was excitement about the successful delivery of the initiative to the entire organization. This should be a time to celebrate the hard work to build trust in the initiative, along with the partnerships developed with the management team and the employees to implement organizational change.

A few minutes after the organizational kick-off meeting was completed, I was told to go to a conference room for a discussion. My belief was that we (my manager, my second level manager, and I) would have a positive conversation about a job well-done; instead, the conversation was focused on a word 'I' that was used during the kick-off meeting.

My manager (while recounting my questionable choice of a word) wagged a finger in my face as if I was a small child who had done something extremely wrong. My manager said, "You said, 'I would like to recognize the first recipient...' instead of saying that 'The organization would like to recognize the first recipient...'."

I was flabbergasted that it was that important to have a closed-door meeting to scold me about the use of the expression "I would like to recognize the ..." versus "The organization would like to recognize the...".

At this moment, I realized that this wasn't a healthy environment in which I would be chastised for the use of the word "I" versus "the organization" during a presentation. Furthermore, it was a little extreme that a closed-door meeting was required for a perceived misstep.

Then, I began to imagine the backlash that might occur for something that was perceived as a major issue. It didn't take me long to determine that pettiness wasn't something that I was willing to endure after several months were spent to diligently prepare to implement a major initiative.

This situation in and of itself wasn't a major issue. The major issue was that there wasn't any recognition for any of the work (performed prior to or during the kick-off meeting) that was positively received by the managers, the project manager, and the organization. Unfortunately, the only focus from my management team was about a trivial issue.

For me, this behavior was a preview of worse things to come, and I wasn't willing to endure shortsighted and shallow management.

Questions

1) After a successful organizational kick-off meeting, what kind of feedback would you expect?

2) What would be your initial thought(s) after being criticized for the use of a word during a meeting?

3) How would you feel if there wasn't any positive feedback for most of the kick-off meeting that went well?

4) Would you remain in the organization? Why or why not?

Lessons Learned

Performance feedback, at times, is misdirected toward perceived flaws instead of a celebration of any success. It is management's responsibility to be supportive of their employees and not be overly critical about trivial matters.

If there's a performance issue, the issue should be addressed with constructive and balanced feedback about ways that things could be done better in the future without being overly critical.

A manager who is overly critical of trivial items can cause more damage than the perceived issue. Therefore, managers should use corrective discussions only for major issues that require course adjustments.

As an alternative feedback mechanism, managers can have their employees complete self-assessments to identify any improvement opportunities. This method is an effective tool for managers and employees to discuss performance issues, challenges, and successes together.

Feedback on minor issues should be left for an employee's self-discovery. Also, (if necessary) a manager can provide minimal, non-formal feedback as a guide for performance improvement.

Otherwise, any positive actions performed by an employee will be under-recognized. Furthermore, this type of management behavior can potentially impact any successes due to an employee's attempt to minimize future negative feedback.

Bullying Behavior Types:
- Coercive
- Positional

Chapter 12:

Quitting Can Have Repercussions

After a little over a year in this organization, solid performance, and the recent completion of my Master of Business Administration (M.B.A.) degree, I was eager to receive a salary increase, which would reflect my job performance and recent educational achievement.

Therefore, a meeting was scheduled with my director to discuss the possibility of a salary increase.

During this meeting, my director communicated that a raise isn't automatically awarded due to the completion of a new educational milestone. The director also informed me that after salary negotiations (at the time of hire), there were limits as to the amount of salary increase that could be given for annual increases or promotions.

My director realized that I was upset by this information. Then, my director advised that the best option to receive a large salary increase was for me to leave the company and return in the future, as this would be the only way that a significant increase could be received at this company.

This advice didn't make sense as it would cost the company more to recruit, on-board, and train someone to fill my position. At this point, I started to search for a new position to receive a salary that was commensurate with my recent educational achievement, skills, and performance.

It took a few months to obtain another position; the director who provided the advice to leave and return to the company to receive a salary increase had left the company.

My new director was an internal hire. This director and I had a good working relationship (at least I thought).

I submitted my customary two weeks' notice after my new director started. My new director wasn't happy that I resigned, perhaps partially due to the timing. This director immediately remarked in a snide manner saying, "This is an interesting situation." My new director went on to say that I should return to their office the next morning.

After returning to work the next morning and ready to start my day, I stopped by my new director's office as requested. Then, I was shocked by the actions that occurred in the next few minutes.

My new director informed me that I didn't need to work my two-week notice period. Then, my director went on to advise that I wouldn't be paid either. This was a shock, as I wanted to work my two-week notice period. Furthermore, working during the notice period was a customary process for an employee who wasn't terminated.

After a consultation with the human resources department about my new director's actions, a human resource representative communicated that my new director was within guidelines.

The human resources representative went on to say that my director had the right to not allow me to work during my notice period.

My next question to the human resources representative was whether I would be paid in lieu of working the notice period, since it was my director's decision that I didn't need to work my notice period. The answer received was "No!"

This was the first time that I was aware of right-to-work laws, which allow any employee or employer to terminate employment at any time for any reason with or without notice.

This unilateral action by my new director was extremely disconcerting, as I was taught that it is professional and responsible behavior to not quit abruptly and provide two-weeks' notice.

I quickly realized that professional and responsible behavior isn't always given in return.

Questions

1) Should an organization allow an employee to work the notice period after a resignation is submitted? Why or why not?

2) What reasons might exist that an employee should not have to work or be paid for the notice period?

3) Were the new director's actions appropriate? Why or why not?

4) What would you do if this happened to you?

5) How might this action impact an employee's actions with future resignations?

Lessons Learned

The inability to work the notice period was a surprise that demonstrated that professional behavior does not always lead to professional behavior in return. The new director's action wasn't a reflection of an employee's ability or performance, but instead a new director's use of power in an inappropriate manner.

The director's behavior was perhaps driven due to a resignation being submitted shortly after their hiring, which may have provoked the director's feelings of a personal insult after assuming the leadership position.

Regardless of the behavior detailed in this case, employees should continue to give proper notice. However, letters of resignation should not be given until the employee is ready to leave because an employer (for whatever reason) may not want an employee to work during the notice period.

Bullying Behavior Types:
- Intimidating
- Positional

Chapter 13:

Overly Reprimanded

I sent an e-mail to a department manager to document the outcome of a meeting. While reviewing my e-mail, my senior manager found a minor typo.

After the discovery, my senior manager lectured me for approximately 10 – 15 minutes about the importance of producing quality documents, along with communicating the importance of the group being represented in the best possible way.

A short time after the meeting, my senior manager sent an e-mail to me to document our discussion. The irony was that my senior manager's e-mail contained typos also.

Questions

1) What would you do if your senior manager advised that an e-mail you sent with a typo does not represent the department in the best way?

2) What would you do if your senior manager sent you an e-mail with typos (after you were reprimanded about the production of quality documents)?

3) Would you inform the senior manager about the e-mail sent with typos? If so, why? If not, why not?

4) How would an e-mail with typos affect your view of the manager (given the previous discussion)?

Lessons Learned

Every issue does not need to be made into a major concern.

A typo in an e-mail can be mentioned to an employee, but there should not be a major issue made about a trivial mistake unless there are ongoing issues.

By making a major issue about an inconsequential matter, a manager's actions can create unintended issues and/or consequences, such as unnecessary stress, slower work performance, etc. Therefore, if an employee makes a mistake an issue should be addressed, but the issue should not be made into a major concern.

This type of issue should be used as an opportunity to teach an employee instead of being an incident that may potentially negatively impact the employee, the manager, and ultimately the department.

Bullying Behavior Types:
- Coercive
- Intimidating
- Positional

Chapter 14:

Working to the Rule

I arrived at my desk, started my computer, and began to unlock my desk around 9:25 a.m. A few minutes later my senior manager walked past my desk as my computer's applications loaded. Then, at approximately 9:45 a.m., I was told to go to my senior manager's office.

After some small talk, I was aggressively informed that employees are expected to be at their desk typing the first keystroke at 9:30 a.m. and not 9:30 a.m. and a second after my start time.

I was baffled by this position as I arrived early, but this wasn't acceptable behavior, even though my official start time was 9:30 a.m.

This extreme position caused me to change my behavior to ensure that my computer was powered on and ready to perform work at 9:30 a.m. and no later.

This unnecessarily strict enforcement caused me to focus on superficial concerns (e.g., the time of my first key stroke). My focus, at times, wasn't directed toward the work because all other work activities were performed cautiously to prevent any other controlling discussions.

After this discussion, I worked to the rule. Therefore, my computer was shut down at exactly 5 p.m. and not 5 p.m. and a second.

This working atmosphere was pathetic, as I would regularly work an hour or so after my shift. However, after this meeting, I decided that if I was held to strict compliance standards, then I would apply strict standards to all areas of my work.

My manager's micro-managing and controlling behavior caused me to expeditiously leave a position I loved. I left this position to seek another internal position due to my manager's tyrannical nature; otherwise, I would've stayed in the position for an indefinite period.

Questions

1) What would you do if your manager insisted that your first key stroke was to occur no later than your exact start time?

2) How might this type of direction affect work performance?

3) Was this manager's expectation reasonable? Why or why not?

4) What are some potential issues that can be created by this type of direction?

Lessons Learned

Strict and arbitrary performance standards can create adverse and unexpected results, which can lead to negative attitudes, work slowdown, or focus on issues other than the work.

Managers should not set strict and arbitrary standards that might unnecessarily impact an employee's performance. Furthermore, managers should not over-manage, but instead provide guidance and course correction.

A manager who gets overly involved with minor infractions might cause their employees to work to prevent future negative consequences instead of a positive focus on the work, including performance excellence.

Managers (particularly those in professional or knowledge-based environments) should allow employees variance from normal standards to complete their job and have a certain level of independence. Otherwise, some employees will feel smothered and leave the environment instead of being put under unnecessary scrutiny and/or duress.

Bullying Behavior Types:
- Coercive
- Intimidating
- Positional

Chapter 15:

Guidance Isn't Always as Received

Direction about work activities is usually initiated from an immediate manager, but at times direction can originate from other members of management. Any such requests that are directed from other managers might not have the same direct authority as that derived from an immediate manager. However, a non-direct report's senior leader's instructions usually must be followed.

An example of this is a matrix manager[6] who directed me to write a critical review of another department's lackluster performance. The matrix manager and I (via our collective analysis of this organization that we had oversight) determined that the leadership style and operational direction were questionable. Then, after further review, my matrix manager told me to create a detailed assessment and send the findings to the department's leader.

It took a few days to complete the analysis and prepare the report. My matrix manager was consulted and involved during the reports' development. Once the report was completed, the report was reviewed and approved by my matrix manager. The report was then sent to the lackluster department director.

A few hours after the report's release, the department's director (whose organization was assessed) wasn't happy with the content and made these views painfully clear.

At this point, my matrix manager created distance between me, the report, and the direction provided to write it. I was now solely held responsible for views that were not flattering but accurate and approved by my matrix manager, along with being left to defend the report's content alone.

---

[6] Matrix Manager – an indirect reporting relationship that allows a manager other than a direct manager to have influence over and/or direct an employee's work activities

The next day my manager held a meeting with all the impacted parties, during which I had to defend the positions in the report alone. My matrix manager who agreed with the report's content was distanced from the report, didn't acknowledge any involvement, and began to criticize the report and me.

After I understood that there wasn't any support for the content or me, I delivered the report's content, answered questions, defended the points, and accepted the public lashing.

This experience was a painful time during my professional career. Although, there were many lessons learned from this experience.

Questions

1) What would you do if this situation happened to you?

2) Should a matrix (non-immediate) manager's direction be followed without approval from an immediate manager?

3) Would you tell your immediate manager that the direction to prepare and issue the report came from the matrix manager? Why or why not?

4) Would your answer to the previous question change if you faced extreme scrutiny for the report's content?

5) Would you communicate to anyone other than your immediate manager that the matrix manager had a critical role in the development of the report's content? If so, when? If not, why not?

Lessons Learned

Constructive feedback can be a challenge to provide and isn't always received in the most positive way. The challenge is to balance the feedback so that the information provided will lead to improvement and not be received as confrontational, condescending, combative, or insulting.

Furthermore, controversial reports that represent an organization's views should be reviewed with the immediate manager and at times with the next level manager prior to release. This additional review will ensure that the organization's position is represented properly and in a manner that's consistent with the leadership's expectations.

In this case, direction was provided by the matrix manager to deliver feedback that was critical of a director's organization's performance.

The report's content should be reviewed with the immediate manager prior to release to ensure that the:

- Immediate manager is informed

- Report is consistent with operational standards

- Immediate manager has an opportunity to review the report's content to be prepared to address or defend any potential issues

Moreover, individuals might not always have another individual's or the organization's interest in mind; therefore, it is very useful to review any potentially controversial positions with an individual's management chain prior to release, as any documents produced reflect the management team and the organization.

Bullying Behavior Types:

- Coercive
- Embarrassing
- Intimidating
- Knowledge
- Manipulative
- Positional

Chapter 16:

Arriving Late and Wanting a Restart

A meeting was scheduled to review a new system application with the business users prior to the application going live. The meeting was going well with the business users until a non-essential user arrived approximately an hour late for the review session.

The person who arrived late wanted the meeting to stop and receive updates on the activities that occurred prior to their arrival.

This person was immediately told that a recap wouldn't be provided at that moment. Furthermore, this individual was advised that a member of my team would be available to schedule a separate review after the meeting. Then, this person became very boisterous about the meeting not being stopped so that a personal update could be received.

After the meeting was brought to a temporary halt, I asked this person who arrived late and disrupted the meeting to follow me into the hallway for a discussion as the meeting continued.

At this point, I explained the reasons that the meeting couldn't be stopped to provide this person with an update. The explanation wasn't received well. Nevertheless, the meeting continued, and the covered material wasn't reviewed just for one person, which was the correct thing to do.

Questions

1) What would you do if someone arrived late to a meeting and wanted a meeting to stop to receive an update on the meeting's activities?

2) Should a meeting be stopped to provide an update to one person? Why or why not?

3) How would you handle a request to stop a meeting and provide someone with a meeting recap, along with the subsequent emotional outburst?

4) Was the removal of the person from the meeting the correct decision? Why or why not?

Lessons Learned

Individuals who arrive late shouldn't be allowed to take-over a meeting and disrespect those who arrived on-time. A request for some (quick) clarification might be appropriate, but it's not reasonable for a meeting to be unnecessarily disrupted and brought to a complete halt (especially for a non-critical business who arrived late).

Moreover, anyone who disrupts a meeting should be removed to prevent an individual from having a negative effect on the flow and potentially the successful outcome of a meeting.

Furthermore, disruptions should be addressed as quickly as possible to resolve the issue and to also not set a precedent for future bad behavior.

Bullying Behavior Types:
- Aggressive
- Coercive
- Condescending

Chapter 17:

It's All About the Money

A company decided to replace its legacy voice mail systems with updated systems that would provide additional features and functionality. The team was early in the planning phase and the extended team was actively involved with requirements definition. The goal was to launch the new voice mail systems in approximately 9 – 12 months.

During the planning phase, the contract was negotiated to meet the most important business needs. It was close to the end of the first quarter and the executive management team provided directions that the contract must be executed prior to the quarter's end. At this point, the team began to work at a quicker pace to meet the given deadline.

Days before the end of the first quarter, an executive manager informed me that in addition to executing the contract, an order for maintenance agreements for all the planned voice mail systems must also be executed. This was of concern to me as the program manager because the equipment wouldn't be installed for approximately nine months. Also, the systems wouldn't be put into service for approximately 2 - 3 months after installation.

My concern was that the voice mail maintenance agreements (if initiated immediately) would be almost or about to expire prior to the first system being installed, which was discussed with my engineering vice president.

The engineering vice president said that my concern was notable, but the direction came from the highest levels of the company and must be followed. The vice president was pressed for an answer about the reasons that direction would be provided to waste company funds. The response provided from the engineering vice president was, "Sometimes we (the company) do stupid things."

My concern was revisited with the engineering vice president a couple of more times until I was directed a second time (against my better judgment) to create agreements to execute maintenance contracts for immediate use for systems that were not yet installed.

My meeting with the engineering vice president was left in frustration as I realized that the company's money (for some unknown reason) would be wasted.

After receiving this direction, I was disgusted with the organization and my engineering vice president because of the lack of justification for the unwarranted voice mail maintenance agreement orders.

Years later, I discovered the reasons for the execution of the maintenance agreements prior to the quarter's end. It was done to book revenue long before the revenue was realized.

Postlude

Prior to a mass layoff, the company which this case is based had an extravagant off-site massive party that was referred to by some as the 'last supper'.

During this event, the company provided rooms of entertainment, along with several theme rooms with lots of different types of foods. A short time after this event, over 1/3 of the workforce nationwide was released on the same day.

Furthermore, the company in this case, along with one of its primary suppliers had a legal complaint filed against it by the Securities and Exchange Commission (SEC), which alleged fraud by both companies.

Questions

1) What would you do if you were told to execute a contract that intentionally wasted money?

2) If company resources are wasted, is it appropriate to report the waste? If so, who should the waste be reported? If not, why not?

3) Does your answer to the previous question change if the direction provided was received from an executive team member? Why or why not?

4) How would this type of direction affect your perception of the company? What about the executive who gave the instruction?

Lessons Learned

It's an employee's responsibility to follow an executive's order(s), unless such instructions are an ethical violation. In such cases, this type of request should be reported directly to a senior level manager, human resources, and/or an anonymous hotline.

It must be noted that a report of a concern directly to the next level management can be risky if there's collusion[7]. Therefore, it is useful to determine and follow company policy to report this type of indiscretion.

If there are concerns about possible retaliation, then the ethical violation(s) should be reported to an anonymous hotline (if available).

It is important that employees not engage in or become involved with hiding unethical activities or providing misleading information, as it is all employees' responsibility to protect company resources from inappropriate actions and/or behaviors.

Bullying Behavior Types:
- Coercive
- Intimidating
- Manipulative
- Positional

---

[7] Collusion – illegally working together on a common goal with an intent to cheat or defraud

Chapter 18:

Power for the Sake of Power

It was around 11:30 a.m. and there were just a few hours before my two week "working vacation." There was a lot to be accomplished before I left the office. My biggest priority was to prepare for an afternoon meeting with my program team, which I was the host.

After the meeting, I planned to return home to pack for my evening flight. As some might imagine, the day was a little bit chaotic and stressful.

At approximately 12:15 p.m., my work was interrupted by someone who was introduced to me and my team members as our new manager. I stopped momentarily to acknowledge and welcome the new manager. Then, I continued to my meeting preparation.

Shortly thereafter, my new manager asked to meet with each team member that day.

During my quick introduction, I advised my new manager that I was in the middle of my preparation for a program status meeting, along with advising that I would leave the office immediately after the status meeting for vacation.

My new manager then asked if I could stop my meeting preparation to get together for about fifteen minutes. My response was, "I really don't have time to meet today, but I could meet with you for about five minutes."

My new manager and I had a brief discussion. As I began to conclude the discussion, I told my new manager that I would be happy to meet for a longer period upon my return from vacation.

At this point, my new manager began to insist that we meet for a longer period before I went on vacation, which I politely declined the request. I then told my new manager again that I needed to finalize material for my upcoming status meeting.

My new manager wasn't pleased, but this wasn't a major issue for me as my reason for not meeting longer that day was clearly explained. Moreover, nobody on the team knew that our new manager was hired until the manager appeared.

After my status meeting was completed, I quickly gathered my belongings and left the office. I didn't have any further thoughts about my discussions with my new manager earlier that day.

During my European vacation, I toured the local attractions until about 4 p.m. local time. After sightseeing, I would go to the local office to work for approximately six hours or so, which allowed me to communicate with my office on U.S. Eastern Time business hours.

My "working vacation" schedule was a challenge. However, this schedule allowed me to manage my program and any critical issues that emerged while on vacation.

I returned home to the U.S. on a Sunday afternoon about a week later. That evening, I received a very unexpected phone call.

A former manager called me to provide advance warning about a change that was made at the office during my vacation. This change was something that a reasonable individual would never expect.

My former manager started with an uncomfortable pause and then told me about an office change, which was made after I left the office. This advance communication was provided by my former manager to prevent me from reacting to the adjustment in the office the next day.

The message delivered caused me to almost drop the phone, and it immediately caused me to yell a few very colorful words.

The urgent message was that my new manager moved me from my desk while I was on my 'working vacation' in retaliation for not meeting with my new manager longer prior to my departure.

The advance warning provided by my former manager was very much appreciated. This notification provided time for me to mentally and emotionally process this egregious act.

As some might imagine, I was enraged and tried to determine the best way to handle this issue. After a good night's sleep, deep thought, and prayer, I went to the office without a clear idea about the way this situation should be handled.

Upon arrival at the office, a co-worker directed me to my new desk in the middle of the floor next to the kitchen in a very high traffic area. This was a significant change from my private window location.

I sat quietly at my new desk, stared at the computer, and contemplated my next steps. After about thirty minutes, a decision was reached. My decision was that I would quit; therefore, I called facilities to bring some boxes to my desk.

After the boxes arrived, I started to pack my books and personal items. I packed about two boxes before my new manager approached and he asked to speak with me, which I agreed. My new manager and I entered a conference room to discuss the relocation from my previous desk, along with my other concerns that led to my decision to leave.

After about an hour, my new manager and I reached an agreement for me to stay.

As for my desk, unfortunately, I was unable to get it back.

Questions

1) Were the new manager's actions reasonable? Why or why not?

2) What would you do if you were moved from your desk while on vacation?

3) How would you handle this situation?

4) Would you agree to continue to work in this group or at this company after the meeting with the new manager? Why or why not?

5) If you agreed to stay, what would be your requirement(s) to stay?

6) Would a pay raise be a significant factor in deciding to stay? Why or why not?

Lessons Learned

Some managers will use whatever power that is available to make a point. For some managers, it may be much more important to make a point than to take time to think about the ramifications of any action on their image.

The biggest lesson learned from this incident is that a manager may have power that is derived from a position; however, a manager does not have power over an individual's response to reckless behavior.

If anyone allows others' actions to affect their response, then the response can be as bad as or worse than the original action. It's always better to respond in a responsible and professional manner. This will help to preserve someone's image and their dignity.

Bullying Behavior Types:
- Aggressive
- Coercive
- Demeaning
- Embarrassing
- Fear
- Intimidating
- Positional

Chapter 19:

It's Only the Contractor

After I started on a new consulting project, I was nervous about my first meeting on this assignment as the project lead.

Most of the attendees attended the first meeting via telephone. Shortly after the meeting started, an individual on the call said to the meeting attendees in a very nasty and aggressive manner, "We don't have to pay attention. It's only the new contractor leading the call."

I was taken back for a moment as this comment was very aggressive and shocking, as this was my first conference call on this assignment.

After I quickly regained my composure, I continued with the call to not let this individual (or anyone in attendance) know that the comments bothered me.

Questions

1) What would you do if you led a call and someone made a comment that nobody needed to pay attention to you during the meeting?

2) Should the comment be addressed? Why or why not?

3) If the comment was addressed, when would the comment be addressed? What would be said about the comment?

Lessons Learned

There's never a good excuse for incivility.

An unfiltered reaction might be to make a comment in response to the outburst; however, any reaction to the unprofessional comment would shift the focus from the meeting's purpose to addressing a personal commentary.

The best option is to ignore the comment unless there are subsequent outbursts. After the meeting, an evaluation can be made as to whether the comment was of a sufficient nature to address or to wait to determine if this was a one-time incident.

The risk is that an overreaction to an isolated outburst (that may not be intended as received) may increase the possibility and risk that the issue might become unnecessarily escalated.

Sometimes, the best approach is to monitor a situation to determine if action is required versus immediately addressing every issue.

At times, a more passive approach can sometimes smooth interpersonal challenges without an escalation of an issue that may otherwise disappear on its own.

Bullying Behavior Types:
- Condescending
- Demeaning
- Embarrassing
- Suggestive

Chapter 20:

This Doesn't Involve You

Bi-weekly status meetings were held to obtain updates on key organizational projects. During this meeting, there were some issues related to the organization's ability to support a new initiative.

Some of the key meeting attendees discussed potential solutions to resolve the issues; at the same time, an individual across from me, who wasn't directly impacted by the changes, tried to provide input into the solution.

At this point, the most senior executive in the meeting slammed a fist on the table and told the individual who provided the unsolicited input, "If I want your opinion, I'll ask for it."

I quickly leaned back in my seat as I thought to myself, "What was that all about?!"

The room suddenly became quiet, but after a brief pause the meeting resumed.

The individual who the executive's comments were directed sat back and didn't speak again during the meeting (this individual didn't speak at any subsequent meetings that I attended).

Questions

1) What would you do if an executive slammed a fist on the table and belittled you in front of a group?

2) Would your answer to the previous question be different if the individual belittled was a colleague instead of you?

3) Is it ever appropriate for an executive to belittle an employee? Why or why not?

4) Was there any action that the meeting attendees could take after a fist was slammed by an executive on the table? Why or why not?

5) How would you react (as the recipient) to the comment, "If I want your opinion, I'll ask for it?"

Lessons Learned

First and foremost, there is never a reason to intentionally embarrass or humiliate anyone. The action that the executive took was unwarranted and out-of-line. An employee attempted to add value via the offered potential solutions and received a nasty response in return.

Executives should be role models of expected behavior from employees. An executive who establishes behavioral standards based on their own inappropriate actions should not be surprised if lower-level employees act similarly.

The organization's culture is driven by the executives' behavior; therefore, executives should showcase the behavior that employees should emulate. Otherwise, there should not be any surprises if there are issues with employees that use similar inappropriate behavior.

Depending on an individual's relationship with the executive, an option could be to ask if any upward coaching can be provided to the executive. If so, the impact of the executive's behavior on the individual, team, and organization can be discussed and hopefully improved.

Bullying Behavior Types:
- Aggressive
- Coercive
- Demeaning
- Fear
- Embarrassing
- Intimidating
- Positional

Chapter 21:

Gifts Can Come

with Expectations

As a program manager on an extremely large organizational project, there were a lot of late-night meetings required to negotiate contractual terms in a very short period. Many times, key members from both teams would dine together and the vendor often paid the bill.

This close relationship was effective to develop solid working relationships; however, the late-night working dinners paid by the vendor had a cost beyond the dinner's price.

Later in the project, there were issues with the approval of a large reorder contract that needed to be executed prior to the last day of the quarter. The reason for the urgency is that the vendor needed the order to meet quarterly revenue objectives. It was at this point that a key executive from this vendor visited my office.

The vendor's executive made it very clear (by looks, tone, and actions) that a debt was due based on past dinners. The executive expected extraordinary effort (on my part) to drive the contract's execution prior to the last day of the quarter.

The contract issues were reviewed to determine if any reasonable assistance could be provided to get the contract signed. However, the vendor wasn't given any extraordinary or preferential treatment.

The support provided wasn't due to the vendor's executive's attempt to strong-arm me based on past activities; the reason that the vendor was assisted was that it was the right thing to do.

After this encounter, my relationship with the vendor's executive was never the same, as my influence isn't available for purchase.

This was the first time in my career that I questioned my judgment and felt dirty by the assumption of quid pro quo.

Questions

1) What are some potential issues that can be created by allowing a vendor to pay for or provide dinners, gifts, or outings?

2) Should there be an expectation of future payback if dinners are paid for by a vendor? Why or why not?

3) What would be your response to the executive's strong-arm position?

4) Should the interaction be reported? If so, to whom?

Lessons Learned

The late-night dinners were considered critical to complete the contract negotiations in an expeditious manner. However, these late night meetings were conducted (from the employee's perspective) without any consideration of future payback.

An individual's perception may not be the reality to another individual. Therefore, it is important to not engage in any questionable behavior or actions that could potentially be viewed as favorable consideration for future business or support.

The removal of any potential for questionable interactions and/or behavior will minimize the opportunity to be put into a situation that could create an unnecessary conflict-of-interest. Furthermore, it is important to disclose any potential conflict-of-interest(s) as soon as possible to minimize any perception of unethical or questionable behavior.

Bullying Behavior Types:
- Coercive
- Connectional
- Intimidating
- Manipulative
- Positional
- Quid Pro Quo
- Suggestive

Chapter 22:

Workers Shouldn't Be Afraid

An organization contracted with me to establish structure, develop standards, and prioritize the organization's projects.

A significant challenge for a project manager is to manage organizational issues, especially on a new engagement. The project manager must carefully balance the responsibility to drive project activities, while also managing resources that are not always under the project manager's direct control.

These challenges can be exacerbated if the management team does not sanction the project manager's authority.

Project managers who do not have organizational support can face threats related to the legitimacy of their authority to outright disregard for the project manager's direction.

An example is an employee who was accustomed to having complete control over their daily work tasks. This type of behavior was very normal for this organization, which appeared to lack a unified and comprehensive direction.

After I requested a project status update from this employee, and during the same discussion, I provided direction about project activities; then, this employee become very emotionally volatile and lashed out at me.

During this outburst, this employee aggressively approached me and assertively entered my personal space. The employee said to me in a very aggressive and immature manner, "I don't have to listen to you; you're not my boss"!

At this point, I very quickly raised my arm and used a stiff-arm stance to prevent this hot-headed individual from getting any closer to me, as I was unsure as to this individual's intentions. My intention, however, was to be prepared to protect myself in the event of a physical attack.

I quickly took a few steps back and said that I would follow-up with the employee's manager about my project directions. Then, I withdrew from the confrontation and returned to my desk to consider the reason for the sudden and explosive outburst.

Questions

1) What challenges might be encountered after a project leadership role is assumed in an organization, which also didn't have any structure to manage projects?

2) How could the challenges identified in the previous question be minimized?

3) What would you do if a colleague approached you in an aggressive manner, along with uncontrolled and emotionally loud outbursts?

4) What action(s) would you take after the incident?

5) What action(s) could be taken to manage the relationship after the incident?

6) Would it be appropriate to seek management's assistance with this emotionally volatile individual? Why or why not?

Lessons Learned

Organizations that initiate change must ensure that the organization's employees are provided with direction, informed, and most importantly directed to support the changes.

Any organizational change that's initiated without a defined rationale for the change (along with employee direction that their support isn't only expected but required) has an increased potential for failure.

By communicating expected behavior, an organization serves notice to its employees that non-compliance won't be tolerated. Furthermore, this type of communication will also provide an opportunity for any issues related to organizational compliance to be dealt with proactively on an individual, departmental, or organizational basis.

Furthermore, employees may be unlikely to support and may create resistance to any change if the organization does not engage employees to provide direction and allow questions to be answered.

As to the person who was overly aggressive and explosive, the time to address extreme levels of aggression and conflict are usually not at the time that the environment is volatile. A better time to deal with an issue is after the situation has calmed, which will provide a better opportunity for both sides to communicate in a relaxed manner.

Anytime an individual in a conflict is worried about a physical confrontation, the primary focus should be to avoid further escalation and to leave the situation as quickly as possible. This will help to reduce the current conflict and minimize the probability of an imminent physical attack.

There aren't any conflicts that are worthy of physical attacks, as there are other options (e.g., request assistance, negotiate a new solution) that can be utilized to resolve the conflict in a calm and purposeful manner.

Bullying Behavior Types:
- Aggressive
- Demeaning
- Direct Comparison
- Fear
- Intimidating

Chapter 23:

Lights Shouldn't Be an Issue

My team recently relocated from another building and received better cubicles near a window. The cubicles were in a great location, but the sun's glare made it very difficult to easily view the computer screen.

Compounding the issue was that many of the team members (including me) would experience eyestrain late in the afternoon. Therefore, the team members seated next to the window decided to work without lights to reduce eyestrain and the glare on the computer screens.

This arrangement worked well until a couple of new employees (who reported to me) moved into the area next to the windows.

One of these employees had vision challenges that made it very difficult to read in a low light environment. This individual was relocated to another area of the office with better lighting. The other new employee remained in the area due to office space challenges. Therefore, my new employee who remained in the area tried to work in a dimly lit environment that was less than optimal for them to see clearly.

At the time the decision was made to work without lights, all team members agreed. However, nobody asked the new team members if this would create any visual challenges for them.

My employee who remained in the area without the lights told me that the lack of lighting impacted their ability to complete work. I said, immediately and without hesitation, "The lights should be 'on' if anyone experienced visual challenges."

The lights were "on" again. Although, all team members weren't happy.

A few days later, a phone call was received (while I was on vacation) from my employee who remained in the area near the window that there was an unsuccessful attempt to turn "on" the lights.

My employee went on to tell me that the lights were turned "on;" shortly thereafter, another employee turned the lights "off."

My employee was so frustrated from the harassment over the lights that the employee said, "Unless you're in the office, I won't come to work."

At this point, my employee's concerns were discussed with our director. Then, my director told the employees in the area that the lights must always be "on" without exception.

The team members adjusted initially, but days later there were still challenges about the lights. It would take another conversation with my director and a team meeting before the lighting issue was finally resolved.

Questions

1) What would you do if you wanted the lights "on" and those seated around you didn't want it?

2) Would you comply with the group's direction to not turn "on" the lights to not create any team conflicts? Why or why not?

3) What would you do to resolve the lighting issue?

Lessons Learned

The actions of the majority don't justify an action, especially if the action(s) impacts or endangers others.

This situation was ridiculous, and the team members acted immaturely and unprofessionally.

The employee who couldn't see properly shouldn't need to battle to have lights turned "on." Moreover, there shouldn't be a need to intervene to have lights "on."

There may be times that appeals to individuals do not work and others' assistance may be required to create change. Therefore, it's sometimes necessary to involve individuals from outside the issue or the organization to build support for a position.

In this case, the director consulted with the building's management about the lights, which led to the lights always being "on" due to a safety hazard. Also, it was a fire code violation to not have sufficient lighting during operating hours.

Bullying Behavior Types:
- Coercive
- Connectional
- Fear
- Intimidating

Chapter 24:
A Waste of Time

I was excited to obtain an interview with a Fortune 100 company. The interview was scheduled for mid-afternoon on a very large corporate campus.

After my car was parked on the company's campus, I had an approximately ten-minute walk to my interview.

Unfortunately, I parked on the wrong side of the campus and the security guard graciously allowed me to cut through the parking garage to enter the correct building.

As I walked through the garage, I received a phone call from the recruiter that advised that my interview was canceled and needed to be rescheduled.

My immediate reaction was disgust and amazement that my interview would be canceled less than twenty-minutes prior to my interview.

The issue that was the most bothersome was that nobody from the company met with me in-person to apologize for the late cancellation, even though I was already on-site.

A few days later, a company representative contacted me to reschedule the interview, which I politely declined.

Questions

1) Is it ever appropriate to cancel an interview within thirty-minutes of the interview? Why or why not?

2) How would you feel if your interview was canceled after you arrived on-site?

3) Were there any alternatives available instead of canceling an interview at the last minute? If so, what? If not, why not?

4) Should someone from a company meet with an interviewee that is already on-site for a short while in-person instead of canceling an interview over the telephone? Why or why not?

5) Would you accept an offer to reschedule the interview? Why or why not?

Lessons Learned

Life happens and sometimes unexpected things occur at the last minute. However, additional consideration should be given to individuals who travel to attend a meeting.

Although it may be disappointing to an attendee that a meeting is canceled, it can be even more upsetting for someone who adjusted their schedule to attend a meeting in-person.

A professional action that should be taken if an interview is canceled with an interviewee already on-site is to (at a minimum) have a company representative meet with the interviewee for a short while. This minor action will demonstrate a high level of professionalism and respect for an individual's time.

The lesson is that others should be treated with the same level of respect that you would want given to you.

Bullying Behavior Type:
- Positional

Chapter 25:

Caught in the Middle

After a few years in my job, I noticed a position posted that could lead to a promotion and a leadership position within this organization. I completed the application process, obtained an interview, and received a job offer for a wonderful opportunity.

My happiness about my job offer was quickly diminished, after I discovered some unexpected news.

After I accepted the job offer, I started to tell colleagues about my promotion. Someone who was told about my promotion wasn't only a friend but was also a mutual friend of another soon-to-be impacted friend and fellow employee.

The friend that was initially told about my promotion was very happy until we (this friend and I) realized that the position I was offered was the job currently held by our mutual friend. My initial (clean version) reaction was, "What just happened?!"

After I considered this unpleasant situation, I began to evaluate the best way to handle it. I didn't know if the mutual friend told the incumbent about the soon-to-be lost position; however, I knew that I had to speak with our impacted friend as soon as possible.

I went to our mutual friend's (the incumbent) office, closed the door, and started to discuss this unfortunate situation. This was a very, very uncomfortable experience, which needed to be addressed immediately and directly.

My friend's response was classy and that of a seasoned professional. My friend didn't blame me or yell at me for the job loss; instead, my friend asked very detailed questions about the situation.

After I obtained some background information about my friend's sudden job loss, my friend (the incumbent) congratulated me on my new position and wished me the best, along with providing me with insights about my new manager. This insight was very useful given the current predicament we just discussed.

The information received related to the job replacement issues, the circumstances that led to the availability of my new position, and the ill treatment of my friend (the incumbent) was never revealed to my new manager.

Questions

1) What would you do if you discovered that your new position was to take the job of a friend who didn't voluntarily leave the position?

2) Would your answer to the previous question change if this same situation happened to you (as the incumbent)?

3) Was it appropriate for the manager to post the position and not tell the incumbent about being removed from the position? Why or why not?

4) Would you discuss the discovery of this issue with the manager who hired you? Why or why not?

Lessons Learned

There will be times that bad situations occur that might put an individual into questionable situations. During these times, it is best to handle the situation quickly and directly, especially if the issue is of a sufficient nature that the issue won't go away. Otherwise, the issue (if not dealt with properly) may lead to further challenges.

The fundamental issue in this case is primarily that of relationship management because:

- The manager mistreated the incumbent by:

    o A failure to manage the employee-manager relationship

    o Not properly and proactively communicating that the individual would be replaced

- The issues were immediately discussed with the friend (the incumbent) to salvage a friendship and to also ensure that the incumbent understood that the job replacement wasn't an underhanded and/or intentional act.

Bullying Behavior Types:
- Coercive
- Demeaning
- Embarrassing
- Intimidating
- Positional

Chapter 26:

Owed a Little Bit of Respect

After being employed for almost two years in an oversight leadership position, the company for which I worked was about to relocate to another area. At this point, all non-essential positions were being eliminated.

My job was included in the eliminated positions, which wasn't a major concern to me given the company's relocation plans. However, the manner in which my position's elimination was handled and communicated was very disrespectful and unprofessional.

I was told to go to my manager's office for a discussion. Shortly after my arrival at my manager's office, I was informed that my position was eliminated effective immediately as part of the planned relocation.

I was then told to pack my office and move to a cubicle on the same floor by the next day. This was a traumatic experience; the day of the meeting I was in a billing leadership position and the next day I was told to call customers to collect money.

This sudden and unexpected change was very impactful as:

- There were not any discussions with me related to other career options

- I had to suddenly report to a new manager

- I was assigned a new job to call customers to collect money, which was something I absolutely didn't want to do

Questions

1) How would you feel if your position was suddenly eliminated without any previous notification?

2) What would you do if your position was suddenly eliminated without any planned options?

3) What would you do if your position was eliminated, and you were assigned a position that you didn't want to do?

4) Should management have inquired about positions that might be preferred first instead of providing an assignment to an unrelated position, which was different than the skill set used in the previous position? Why or why not??

Lessons Learned

Individuals always have control over their career options regardless of choices others may make for them. However, if someone works for another, then there will always be someone that has influence over their career, opportunities, and future.

Just because someone has influence over an individual's career, this doesn't mean that the influence should be used (especially to the detriment of another).

If decisions are made related to someone's career, the individual(s) making the decision(s) should (to the extent possible) involve the impacted party in the career decision.

Otherwise, there might be resentment about the decision, which could lead to performance issues, behavioral challenges, or the impacted employee may leave the company.

It's important to remember that business decisions can be communicated and implemented in a manner that minimizes the impact to the most important resources... the employees.

Bullying Behavior Types:
- Demeaning
- Positional

Chapter 27:

Too Important
to Acknowledge

A decision was needed from a functional director just prior to a product launch. Therefore, I went to the director's office to obtain a timely decision. The door was open. The director was in the office, but there was another person in there also.

Normally, I would return later if there was a meeting, especially if the door was closed. In this case, a timely decision was required, and the door was open.

I waited at the office door to be acknowledged, but the director refused to acknowledge my presence, perhaps because I was a consultant. I waited a minute, five minutes, and almost ten minutes, but the director refused to acknowledge my presence.

At first, I thought that the director wanted to wait until a break in the conversation to acknowledge me. Then, I realized that the director was determined to not acknowledge my presence (not even for a minute).

After waiting for almost ten minutes, I interrupted the discussion and told the director that a time sensitive decision was required to not impact the product launch. The director finally acknowledged me and said, "I will contact you later" in a condescending tone.

At first, the reason that I waited at the director's office door was to obtain a timely decision. Then, I waited to determine the amount of time it would take for this director to not acknowledge my presence.

This director refused to acknowledge my presence with verbal or non-verbal cues, until I finally interrupted the director's conversation.

Delayed input was ultimately received from the director. However, the input was only provided after the incident was reported and handled by my on-site manager.

Questions

1) What would you do if you visited an office and the person in the office refused to acknowledge you?

2) How much time would you give someone to acknowledge your presence prior to interrupting a discussion? Why is this amount of time appropriate?

3) Is it appropriate to interrupt a discussion in progress? Why or why not?

4) Is it appropriate to interrupt a discussion for a meeting that is underway with the door open? Why or why not?

Lessons Learned

Interrupting a meeting in progress is generally not a good habit; however, there are times that decisions are required that are time sensitive and require a meeting to be interrupted.

Normally, an open-door meeting is subject to interruption after a party to the in-progress conversation acknowledges the visitor. As for a closed-door meeting, the meeting should not be interrupted unless there is an immediate need.

If there is an immediate need to interrupt a closed-door meeting, the individual who requires information should knock on the door, wait a moment to be acknowledged, and then enter.

Generally, if someone arrives while a conversation is in progress, then it's customary for someone in the conversation to acknowledge the visitor(s).

Respectful actions include:

- Inquiring about the reason for the visit

- Asking the visitor(s) to wait

- Requesting the visitor(s) to return later if the current discussion cannot be interrupted

It's never acceptable to ignore someone who purposely visits for a discussion. Someone who visits an office should be given even greater consideration, as the person personally visited (not e-mailed or called) to have a face-to-face discussion for a reason.

Furthermore, there is never an excuse for rude behavior. Individuals should be treated with the same level of respect as they would want for themselves.

Bullying Behavior Types:
- Condescending
- Demeaning
- Intimidating
- Positional

Chapter 28:

Don't Yell at

My Employees

My employees worked at an offsite location to be closer to the development team just prior to the system release date. These employees complained that an Information Technology (IT) manager created a stressful environment for them due to being overly critical of their work.

Based on the employees' report, I decided to spend a little more time at the offsite location to ensure my employees were not being harassed. This was an issue that required my immediate attention as this IT manager had a pattern of less than professional behavior.

After I got close to my employees' work area, I overheard a very loud conversation that originated from the room in which my employees worked. The very loud noise originated from the very aggressive IT manager who was yelling at my employees.

After I entered the room, I immediately asked to speak with the IT manager outside the room. Our conversation was about the IT manager's aggressive behavior toward my employees, along with a conversation about role clarity to ensure that the IT manager understood that these employees reported to me. Furthermore, the IT manager was also told not to yell at my employees again.

This conversation served notice to the IT manager that direction for my employees work activities should and would originate from me and not the IT manager.

The IT manager didn't appreciate the conversation; however, it was essential that I communicated to the IT manager that I was the only manager for my team.

Questions

1) Is it ever appropriate for a manager to yell at their team? Why or why not?

2) What would you do if a manager yelled at your team as you arrived?

3) Is there ever a reason that another manager (especially someone who does not have a reporting relationship with a team) should yell at a team? Why or why not?

4) What instructions would be given to your team about addressing similar issues in the future?

5) What message would you convey to a manager who yelled at your team?

Lessons Learned

Managers should not yell at their employees. This is especially true for a manager who does not have a reporting relationship with the employees. Regardless, a manager's job is to protect and insulate their team from organizational politics, unnecessary stress, and volatile or hostile work environments.

Any manager who has an issue with another team's performance should address any issue with the team's manager and not the individual team members. This will allow the manager with concerns to seek clarification about the team's reason(s) for their performance; otherwise, unnecessary conflict can be created between a manager with a concern, the employees, the manager, the team, and/or the organization.

It is useful to follow reporting relationships whenever there is a need to address and/or adjust a team's or an employee's performance, especially if there isn't a direct reporting relationship.

Bullying Behavior Types:
- Aggressive
- Coercive
- Condescending
- Demeaning
- Fear
- Intimidating
- Positional
- Reputational

Chapter 29:
Your Strength
Doesn't Intimidate

There is a great opportunity to make a lot of money as an independent consultant, but the money does not always make up for the sometimes-aggressive behavior and bad treatment that consultants may experience.

On this particular contract, the client selected a vendor and was about to begin an implementation that would last approximately six months. However, after a few days on-site with the client, the implementation changed from a potentially reasonable approach to a quick descent into disarray.

The vendor selected for the implementation didn't receive any requirements; nevertheless, the client wanted the implementation completed by the end of the current month.

The correct approach should have been to implement the new system using project management methodology; instead, the client directed the system implementation to be completed by the end of the month without requirements, a disregard for the lack of any employee training, and other factors.

This system was implemented under fire!

This implementation was the sloppiest, most disorganized, and the worst system development project with which I had the misfortune of being associated. However, I appreciate a challenge; therefore, I did the best job possible given the circumstances.

My hope was that this chaotic implementation would be a one-time incident, but unfortunately the chaos associated with my first project in this organization wasn't an isolated event.

The next project assigned wasn't as hectic, but it was still very bad due to management's inability to make a decision and/or understand the scope of work.

Another concern was that the business project manager was an absolute nightmare to work with on this project. The business project manager wanted to direct the project, but this individual didn't understand the technology, the process changes required, and most importantly the human aspect due to the sensitive nature of the system changes.

For example, if an approach or decision was made that was counter to the business project manager's opinion, the business project manager would literally have a temper tantrum.

Imagine working in a professional environment with a team member who would issue threats every time an approach and/or a decision didn't meet their expectations.

The project's goal was to meet the business' needs; however, decisions should not be made for the sake of an individual getting their way, especially at the expense of meeting the needs of the business and/or project.

The challenge of dealing with the business project manager was a nightmare, which often led to unnecessary discussions, meetings, communication, etc. Furthermore, decisions were often delayed because the technical team didn't have much leverage to override the business project manager's whims and unrealistic demands.

Furthermore, the technical team had to prove and argue about every technical decision with an individual who didn't understand the technology. Nevertheless, the team tried its best to accommodate every request from the business project manager, but these ongoing challenges and battles began to exhaust the team and me (as the project manager).

After a few too many confrontations from an unyielding business project manager and an inability to make forward progress due to this individual, I decided (based on this project and past experiences) that this was an unhealthy and unproductive place to work.

The on-site management team was informed by me about the ongoing challenges with the business project manager. Moreover, I also believed that the organizational disarray wouldn't improve; therefore, my on-site manager was informed that I would leave the organization.

After my resignation was received, my on-site manager met with me to try to convince me to stay, which I reluctantly agreed.

The reason that I stayed was that this was a critical project for the organization, and I didn't want to leave the team in a bad position. However, this project environment continued to deteriorate due to management's refusal to make strategic decisions and the end-users started to revolt due to some recent executive decisions.

All these factors and more led to continuous challenges with setting project direction. Furthermore, I was held responsible for successful program delivery; however, my program team's collective decisions were often overridden by a controlling business project manager.

Being tired of the ongoing unnecessary battles with the business project manager who didn't understand the technology, but wanted to force an unrealistic and uneducated solution, along with the executive team's reluctance to provide strategic direction or make any decisions. Therefore, I decided to resign again.

This time my manager asked me to meet with the organization's senior executive. This was the strangest meeting of my career.

After I entered the senior executive's office, I shook hands with this senior executive (who for some strange reason that still leaves me bewildered) who squeezed my hand so hard that my fingers collapsed upon each other.

The senior executive didn't make my knees buckle, but this executive squeezed my hand so hard that I was on the verge of my body starting to respond to the vice-grip. This encounter left me very perplexed, but my feelings were suppressed and softened a little due to the receipt of a generous raise to stay.

After some soul searching, even with the raise, I decided to leave this position after my contract expired a few weeks later.

A reason for my departure was that the salary increase wouldn't correct the excessive organizational issues. Moreover, as a consultant my impact was limited unless the organization gave me the necessary authority to make the required decisions and changes.

The main reason I left this engagement was due to the chaotic environment, which was driven by a lack of executive leadership and a domineering business project manager. The secondary reason I left was my encounter with a senior executive who would intentionally try to intimidate anyone by excessively squeezing a hand to create physical pain.

Questions

1) What would you do if an organization's representative forced a position or direction without the expertise to make the best decision?

2) How would you handle an individual who constantly throws a temper tantrum?

3) What would you do if an executive squeezed your hand beyond reasonable standards?

4) Would you tell anyone about your hand being squeezed excessively? If so, who and why? If not, why not?

5) Would your answer to the previous question change if you were a consultant? Why or why not?

6) Would you say anything about the hand squeezing to the executive who squeezed your hand excessively? If so, why? If not, why not?

7) Would you remain in the organization after a pay raise was received? Why or why not?

8) Do you agree with the reason for the departure at the end of the contract term? Why or why not?

Lessons Learned

The biggest challenge (as an independent consultant) is often related to relationship management. The reason is that independent consultants can have less protection from organizational politics or questionable behavior than a company's employees.

Therefore, consultants are less likely to report unreasonable, unfair, inappropriate, or abusive work environments due to a fear of job and/or pay loss. These types of fear can be powerful motivators to remain silent about workplace challenges, as a consultant or an employee.

Company employees are generally protected from sudden employment losses due to documented human resource policies, which must be followed.

For independent consultants, an assignment can be terminated without any warning, documentation, or opportunity for improvement.

Moreover, consultants can be (and often are) held to higher performance standards. The general expectation is that consultants will get up-to-speed quickly and be able to meet performance expectations almost immediately. This can be a significant challenge especially while dealing with clients who have unreasonable and unrealistic expectations, lack of direction, or organizational chaos.

Furthermore, project issues can be managed, changed, or eliminated; however, the lack of executive direction is very difficult to change, especially for an independent consultant.

Teams need leaders who can make timely decisions to ensure activities continue to proceed. Moreover, it is a good habit to get employees engaged in the decision-making process to the extent possible. This involvement will increase the likelihood that employees will support activities or actions for which their assistance was provided during the decision-making process.

Although, there are times that executives must make tough and sometimes unpopular unilateral decisions. In these times, executives should survey impacted employees to gauge responses to the proposed changes and to also obtain a different perspective. This may increase employee support for an effort, even if the employee's preferred choice isn't selected. This guidance will generally work if management communicates the reason(s) for the decision.

As for the use of physical strength against anyone in an organization, this should never be tolerated.

Moreover, any abuse (e.g., physical, mental, emotional, otherwise) should be reported (although not done for this example) because there may be other unreported incidents. If an incident isn't reported, then there isn't a record of the incident to document a pattern of abusive behavior becomes more difficult to prove.

Furthermore, money may temporarily make an individual feel a little better, but money won't change the environment. Money may help to temporarily defer an individual's attention, but this diversion won't change the issues that created the original situation if the specific issues are not addressed.

Therefore, money isn't always the answer!

Bullying Behavior Types:
- Aggressive
- Coercive
- Intimidating
- Physical
- Positional

Chapter 30:

Cost of Staying Connected

One of the toughest contract assignments that I had was partially due to some unexpected life challenges outside of work.

During this assignment, my Achilles tendon was torn, my mom broke her hip (so I was in the nursing home before and after work). Also, I took care of my mom after her release from the nursing home, I had the flu for almost two weeks, and then I developed a case of pinkeye.

It was a rough four-month period. My on-site manager and director were aware of my personal challenges outside of work, which allowed me to balance my performance and family commitments during this chaotic period.

The toughest period on this assignment was working almost a full day while sick with the flu to drive program issues just prior to a system release going into production. While sick, I used my company issued mobile phone more than normal to remain connected to the project team.

A little over a month after my illness, a meeting with my on-site manager and me was held to discuss my previous month's (higher than normal) mobile phone charges.

During this period, an additional focus was placed on all mobile phone bills because a new executive was working aggressively to reduce operating costs (due to an increasingly challenging economic climate).

It is important to emphasize that my previous month's phone bill was higher than normal during my illness. Also, there were not any previous issues with excessive mobile phone bill charges.

The organization scrambled to explain my mobile phone bill cost, especially since I was a consultant.

Normally, organizations will select mobile plans that allow for the greatest amount of flexibility because the cost of exceeding plan minutes can be very expensive. However, the individual who ordered the mobile phone for me selected a cheaper price plan versus factoring the potential for higher monthly bills if the price plan allowance was exceeded.

My manager asked me to check with the purchasing office to determine if the mobile phone plan could be retroactively changed to reduce my phone bill cost, which the answer later received was 'no'.

Furthermore, there was a question about my decision to not use my home landline phone, which was quickly terminated after I revealed that I didn't have a landline phone that could be used. This commentary left me speechless because I kept the program moving forward while I barely had enough strength due to having the flu.

I was very perplexed by this conversation, as I didn't understand the reason that I would even have to justify the use of a company mobile phone for company business versus the use of a personal landline phone for company business.

The manner in which this situation was handled caused me to reevaluate my decision-making process that would put my work ahead of my health.

Questions

1) Was it appropriate for the manager to focus on the cost of the phone bill versus a resources' health?

2) How would you handle a discussion about a one-time mobile phone cost overrun?

3) Should someone work during an illness (even if the program was at a critical period)? Why or why not?

4) Whose responsibility should it have been to deal with the purchasing department about the acquisition of a different price plan (the consultant, the on-site staff, or someone else)?

5) Would the handling of this situation effect your future performance? Why or why not?

Lessons Learned

A job will usually continue long after a resource (e.g., employee, consultant) is no longer on the job. Therefore, resources should prioritize their health as more important than a job and a paycheck.

Organizations may not always be concerned about a resource's challenges outside of work. However, resources should always prioritize accordingly. The priority for resources is to themselves and family; then, secondary concerns should be given to work responsibilities.

Bullying Behavior Types:
- Coercive
- Positional

Chapter 31:

Your Performance
Will Be Graded

While in search of a new opportunity, I was contacted to interview for an exciting contract opportunity. This position had great potential for career advancement, but my dreams about this potentially rewarding career adventure quickly turned to angst during the interview.

The interview progressed in a normal manner. There were brief introductions, general overviews, and then the interview. The interview proceeded well and there appeared to be interest on both sides.

The interview then took an unexpected turn. The task lead began to detail the on-site manager's operating practices, which included the client manager's assignment of letter grades to the consultants each week based on performance.

My immediate thought was, "Are you kidding me?! This has got to be a joke." Unfortunately, it wasn't a joke, and it was about to get worse.

Later during the interview, the task lead said that the on-site manager would at times make very abrupt, attacking, and sometimes insulting comments during a meeting if the client manager wasn't happy with someone's performance.

This information made my decision to not accept the position a lot easier.

Questions

1) Is it appropriate for a manager to evaluate an employee's performance weekly? Why or why not?

2) Is it appropriate for a manager to assign a letter grade to an employee's performance weekly? Why or why not?

3) Would knowledge that a client manager would assign a letter grade to your performance weekly affect your decision to accept a job? Why or why not?

4) Is it ever appropriate for a manager to provide negative individual performance feedback in a group setting? Why or why not?

Lessons Learned

An early warning about potential behavior that is outside customary boundaries and/or overly controlling should be an immediate concern.

Resources (e.g., employees, consultants) deserve to receive timely feedback; however, feedback should be given periodically to allow resources an opportunity to learn, grow, and manage their performance. Otherwise, resources may be under continuous fear of the receipt of a negative performance appraisal instead of maintaining focus on excellent performance.

Work should not be a playground, but it also should not be an environment for resources to be overly concerned about being excessively evaluated and/or rated.

It is a leader's responsibility to provide feedback that is useful to adjust or improve performance. Furthermore, performance feedback should not be used as a constant threat or weapon that might have negative consequence(s).

Managers should be supportive of their resources and provide guidance for performance improvement, which if done correctly can lead to sustained performance.

It is important to remember to "praise individuals in public and punish in private."

Bullying Behavior Types:

- Coercive
- Condescending
- Fear
- Intimidating
- Positional
- Reputational

Chapter 32:

Sounding the Alarm

At times, quick decisions are required to prevent delays with work activities.

On this project, a project director's input was required on a business decision. The director didn't respond to my e-mails or voice mails. Therefore, I decided to visit the director's assistant to obtain a quick response.

The director's assistant was visited to attempt to determine the best method to contact the director to obtain an immediate decision about an important issue.

Shortly after the question was asked, the assistant without any warning slammed a fist on the desk and said, "You don't know everything that is going on at my desk."

At this point, I was a little concerned and bothered by the response. Therefore, I retreated from the area quickly to not become involved in a confrontation.

The next morning, upon arrival to the office, I noticed a package on my desk. The package was a gift that was left by my director's assistant, along with an apology note for the previous day's behavior.

Questions

1) What would you do if a colleague or manager became aggressive during a discussion?

2) Is it ever appropriate to use physical aggression to make a point? Why or why not?

3) What actions could be taken to diffuse a similar situation?

5) Should any action be taken after the confrontation? Why or why not?

6) How might this unexpected aggressive behavior affect future interactions with this individual?

Lessons Learned

There are different ways to express dissatisfaction or stress without the use of aggressive gestures. Therefore, it's never appropriate for anyone to use physical or verbal aggression to attempt to intimidate another.

Once someone becomes emotionally and/or physically aggressive, the best action is to withdraw from the situation. This action will allow all parties time to have an opportunity to calm down and reflect on the situation. Otherwise, there's an opportunity for a situation to escalate and quickly become a much larger issue immediately, as well as in the future.

Bullying Behavior Types:
- Aggressive
- Fear
- Intimidating

Chapter 33:

The Customer

Isn't Always Right

I completed a "draft" audit report, which was presented to an external client without any issues identified. At this point in the audit cycle, the report is generally considered a final version.

A few weeks later, the "final" audit report was completed and was ready to be delivered to the client. However, due to budgetary challenges the client wanted key elements of the report changed to meet its budgetary needs.

The issue with the client's request was that the independent audit results didn't justify the changes. Therefore, my executive team's (for the company which I worked) support and approval was received to not materially change the audit results to meet the client's needs.

After my executive team's approval was received, the client's request to adjust the audit results to meet its budget and/or political needs was rejected.

A few weeks later, the client tried again to have the audit results changed; this request was also rejected. At this point, the executive team was still in agreement that the audit results should not be altered.

A short time later, the client insisted in a more forceful manner that the report must be changed to meet its needs. At this moment, my executive team continued to support me and agreed that the report shouldn't be changed.

Then, the client dictated that if the report wasn't changed to reflect its needs, there wouldn't be any potential for future business (the company would be "blacklisted").

My executive team then directed me to change the audit results to meet the client's needs. This direction was provided so that the company wouldn't lose future business with a significant revenue contributor.

After this direction was received to change the independent audit results to reflect information other than the observations made by me during the audit, I decided to resign instead of having to submit a report (under my name) with data that didn't reflect the actual results, along with having manipulated information.

Moreover, the audit report if I stayed would list my name as the report's author and not the company; therefore, I didn't want my name associated with unethical behavior.

> Note: I was the only individual from the company who was authorized and certified by the client to submit the audit report for this contract. This explicit authorization was given because the client wanted the audit and the report to be completed by an individual with very specific credentials.

It was unethical for the audit results to be manipulated, as the audit was contracted as an independent audit.

Furthermore, I (as the audit lead) didn't agree to make any material adjustments to the audit report, especially any changes that were made to meet the client's budgetary and/or political objectives.

After I resigned, an executive told me that I no longer needed to come to the office; although, the executive wanted me to be available during my two weeks' notice period, to which I agreed.

Unfortunately, the agreement was revoked a couple days prior to the end of my notice period because the company received the information it needed from me to submit the audit report.

At this point, I was told to report to the office with my company issued equipment the next day.

After I reported to the office, I was informed by an executive that this was my last day. I was also told that I wouldn't be paid for the last couple of days. I was upset by the decision to not pay me for the last few days; however, I decided that it wasn't worth getting into an argument.

As I was about to leave the building, the same executive (who moments before told me that I wouldn't be paid) wished me good luck and then gave me a hug.

This hug was a very awkward, uncomfortable, and weird moment.

Questions

1) What would you do if a client asked you to change an audit report to something that didn't reflect the actual audit findings?

2) What role does management have to ensure ethical compliance and/or behavior?

3) What would you do if your management team asked you to change audit results to something that the audit results didn't reflect?

4) Is it ever acceptable to manipulate results to meet a client's needs? Why or why not?

5) Would your answer to the previous question change if your name is listed as the author of an audit report? Why or why not?

6) Was it appropriate for the executive to not pay the salary for the last couple of days? Why or why not?

7) Was it appropriate for the executive to offer and give a hug on the last day after moments earlier advising that salary wouldn't be paid for the last couple of days? Why or why not?

Lessons Learned

Resources (e.g., employees, consultants) should operate in good faith in business activities and should not be a party to unethical behavior. It is an organization's responsibility to establish behavioral standards for all employees to follow and comply; otherwise, employees (including executives) may use discretionary practices to determine whether standards should be followed and/or are ethical.

Furthermore, organizations should not only provide ethical guidance, but there should also be documented ethical compliance standards to ensure that any opportunities for unethical behavior are minimized.

Some of the most important factors in ethical behavior are:

- The manner that executives demonstrate ethical standards

- Controls to ensure enforcement

- The opportunity to engage in illicit activities

If employees observe that either executives are not modeling the expected ethical behavior and/or there is an opportunity to not get caught engaging in unethical behavior, then the perceived and actual risk of being caught is minimized. Therefore, executive management must set standards and demonstrate the behavior(s) in which a company's ethical policies are based.

Bullying Behavior Types:

- Coercive
- Knowledge
- Positional
- Withholding

Chapter 34:

Responding Shouldn't Be That Hard

I received an offer for a senior level position; however, the offer was contingent on a contract that would be awarded in a few months.

This offer was for a very senior position that was worth the wait to receive, but not at the cost of the loss of another opportunity with an immediate bona fide offer.

Therefore, the contingent employment offer was countered with a request for a signing bonus to provide an incentive to justify the wait for the position just in case the contract wasn't awarded to the company.

After my request was made for a signing bonus, there wasn't any further communication received from the company (even after several voice mails were left for the human resource manager).

Questions

1) Was the request for a signing bonus appropriate given that other opportunities could be lost to wait for a contract that wasn't guaranteed? Why or why not?

2) Was it appropriate for the organization to not respond to the counteroffer? Why or why not?

3) What would you do if an offer was provided and then upon making a counteroffer there wasn't any further contact?

Lessons Learned

If a company believes that an employment counteroffer isn't reasonable or does not want to accept it, this should be communicated to the applicant.

It is important to note that contingent offers are not actual offers; therefore, parties to a contingent offer must take steps to protect their interest until there is a signed contract. Otherwise, other offers may be foregone while an individual waits for an opportunity that might not ever materialize.

Anyone who doesn't have the common courtesy to return a phone call (to advise that the terms offered aren't acceptable) is someone who isn't worth doing business with anyway.

The actions taken at the beginning of a relationship are often indicative of future behaviors once the relationship is developed.

Bullying Behavior Types:
- Demeaning
- Intimidating
- Positional

Chapter 35:

Your Time Isn't as Valuable

After I arrived for an interview, I was escorted to the recruiter's desk to wait for my interview that was scheduled to begin in about fifteen minutes. At about ten minutes before the hour, the recruiter led me to a conference room.

Once we reached the conference room, the recruiter went into the room and returned rather quickly to communicate that none of the interviewers had arrived. Then, the recruiter called the interviewers, but nobody could be contacted.

I waited in the hallway for approximately 10 - 15 minutes as the recruiter scrambled to locate the three interviewers. While I waited, I started to become anxious and suggested to the recruiter that my interview should be rescheduled, but the recruiter didn't concur.

After I had already stood in the hallway for 20 - 25 minutes, the first interviewer arrived at the conference room. The recruiter then went into the conference room for approximately five minutes, while I continued to wait in the hallway.

This lack of courtesy and professionalism was ridiculous!

The recruiter returned and informed me that another manager was contacted to interview me. The last-minute addition of an interviewer and an interviewer missing didn't give me a great feeling, as I had now waited in the hallway for approximately thirty minutes.

At this point, I asked (and almost pleaded with) the recruiter for my interview to be rescheduled so that I could have the best opportunity to get the job. However, my request was discounted and ignored, as the recruiter continued to try to locate interviewers.

This interview experience was a fiasco because of the three original interviewers: one was present, one was absent, and the replacement hadn't reviewed my credentials.

Almost forty-five minutes after my interview was scheduled to begin, my interview started, but the interview didn't last ten minutes.

After some small talk, there was a technical question from an interviewer (who didn't review my resume) that I didn't answer properly. My answer was slightly incorrect because I couldn't remember all the process steps for the question asked, which might be partly due to my frustration related to standing in the hallway for almost an hour.

The technical question was only a part of the interview. Therefore, the unscheduled interviewer could have asked questions related to my strengths in managing projects as this job was primarily a program management position.

Unfortunately, after an excessive delay, my interview was over without recourse.

After waiting for almost an hour for my interview to begin, my interview was over after a single question was asked by an individual who was sought at the last minute to interview me.

As I left the room, the two interviewers, especially the interviewer who wasn't scheduled to be in the room, were smiling in a sly manner. This occurred shortly after my interview was abruptly terminated due to my partially incorrect answer to a question.

The part that is the most troublesome is that the question asked by the unscheduled interviewer wasn't directly related to the job or my skill set as a Project Management Professional (PMP).

Questions

1) What would you do if the interviewers were not ready for an interview?

2) How long would you wait for the interview to begin? Why would you wait for this amount of time?

3) Did the recruiter act appropriately? Why or why not?

4) Should the interview have been rescheduled? Why or why not?

5) Would you wait thirty minutes or more for an organization to scramble to find individuals to interview you? Why or why not?

6) What might the interview scheduling challenges suggest about the organization?

7) If you were invited back to interview (after the first experience), would you return? Why or why not?

Lessons Learned

Everything isn't within your control. At times, an individual can be fully prepared and still fail.

A failure at a single moment isn't an indication of a failure of an individual, as there are generally multiple factors that can influence whether a momentary event is successful or not.

This situation was headed for a potentially bad start and conclusion from the beginning. Whenever anyone is scrambling to find individuals or resources, there is a potential for unexpected results.

Moreover, individuals will sometimes use situations to provide themselves with a feeling of superiority and/or control.

The unscheduled interviewer could have made the situation more comfortable by simply referencing the uncoordinated and chaotic events prior to the interview. However, the unscheduled interviewer's focus appeared to be to determine (via an artificial and very limited measurement with a single question) if the interviewee wasn't qualified versus determining if there was a good fit. This type of arbitrary evaluation isn't a fair litmus test of an applicant's ability.

Anyone who uses their power just because it's available (instead of needed) communicates more about themselves rather than the target of the power. Therefore, power should be used because it's needed and not just because it is available.

Bullying Behavior Types:
- Coercive
- Positional

Chapter 36:

The Power is Mine to Use

The assumption of a difficult program in the middle can be a huge challenge; however, assumption of program leadership as a consultant can be even more of a challenge, as the expectations for consultants can generally be a lot higher than that for employees.

Adding to the complexity of this program was the intertwined management and funding relationships. The organization that contracted my services managed my day-to-day activities, but the funding for my services came from a program sponsor in another organization.

This type of arrangement can be an enormous challenge if the environment and the relationships are not managed carefully.

On this program, this organization gave me the responsibility and the authority to manage the program as needed.

This organization's employees were committed and eager for the program implementation that would lead to improved system efficiency and effectiveness. The biggest program challenge was my ability to manage a significant number of resources in and outside the organization, especially the program sponsor.

As a customary practice, the key stakeholders were consulted on the vision, requirements, action items, and program risks. The program was managed in a very open style so that all key stakeholders felt comfortable. This created a collaborative environment in which everyone had opportunities to provide input on program activities.

The first time I was concerned about the program sponsor was during a meeting to resolve key issues prior to a program status meeting. The team worked on an issue for a while and developed a reasonable approach to resolve the issue. Then, late in the meeting the program sponsor arrived.

The program sponsor started to detail the very senior-level managers with whom this person met with prior to the meeting, which impacted the sponsor's ability to arrive at the start of the meeting. This pattern of behavior would continue throughout the contract engagement.

The late arrivals, name-drops, disruptions, and the attempts to take-over meetings were dealt with by me professionally; although, at times, I had a strong desire to tell the program sponsor, "Okay, we get it; you're important!", but with lots of self-control I always suppressed this internal dialogue.

The program sponsor also had a bad habit of making late comments on project decisions, which created a lot of additional work to justify the decisions reached by the stakeholders that met the deadlines. These types of issues were manageable, but the behaviors that followed were beyond the standards of common courtesy and decency.

For example, there was a meeting in the main cafeteria. The program sponsor was at a table that seated approximately four (4) individuals. Upon my arrival at the table, I asked the sponsor and the individuals who arrived with me to move to a larger table to accommodate the expected number of meeting attendees.

Shortly after making the request, the program sponsor yelled at me about my request to change tables in a tone that I seldom use with my dogs.

After being yelled at in a very unprofessional manner, I immediately walked away. If I stayed in the area, then I would've become involved in a confrontation and said something inappropriate.

> Note: The protection for a consultant isn't as great as for employees. Therefore, a consultant must be even more careful with their behavior because consultants can be terminated with a lot less hassle and paperwork than an employee.

Regardless, I left the area. Then, I called a consultant who worked for me (and was also in the area during the verbal confrontation) to have a quick, private conversation.

My consultant was at the table with the program sponsor. I called my consultant who answered the phone and said 'hello'. My consultant then said my name, which made me a little frustrated. My frustration during this call was because I wanted to discuss the incident with my consultant, cool down, but not let the sponsor know that I asked my consultant to walk away from the table to speak with me.

After a small delay to regain my focus on the meeting's purpose, I continued the meeting as scheduled. This incident and unnecessary attack would be representative of many uncomfortable encounters that occurred between me and the program sponsor during my contract tenure.

This incident and others were reported by me to my on-site director to address; however, my director was very passive and didn't like confrontations. Therefore, the director didn't and wouldn't address the bullying behavior I reported, perhaps partly due to being afraid of the program sponsor.

Fast forward to late in the program, I was about to complete my program activities and was a little tired due to an incredibly challenging but personally rewarding program experience.

At the end of the program, there were some issues that wouldn't be resolved prior to my assignment's completion. Therefore, I wanted to exert effort to make significant progress on several issues prior to exiting the program and the contract.

After the program sponsor discovered that I was working on an issue per the instruction of my on-site director, I was aggressively and assertively told by the sponsor that my support wasn't wanted nor needed. Then, I immediately told the sponsor that my direction and priorities came from my on-site director and not the sponsor.

At this point, the program sponsor reminded me (as it was done throughout the assignment) that the approval of the funding for my services came from the sponsor's organization.

This conversation with the program sponsor was reported to my on-site director, as the others were reported also. My on-site director, after this conversation was disclosed, instructed me to continue to work as normal.

Around the same time, I was about to finish my contract responsibilities, there was a meeting to discuss some post-implementation program issues.

During this meeting, the program sponsor was seated to my right. As we discussed the issues (the same way issues were discussed throughout the program), I made a comment, and the sponsor spoke over me. Then almost immediately, the sponsor turned to position their back to me, as to indicate that your comments are not important or wanted.

The program sponsor's actions were ignored at first by everyone, including me until I made another comment. This time, the sponsor became more aggressive and spoke over me again. At this point, I received a clear signal about the sponsor's intent and decided to not actively participate in the meeting any further.

After the meeting, I had a conversation about the incident with the individual with whom I worked with the closest during the contract.

Our conversation was about the program sponsor's actions during the meeting. After all the abuse and hostility during the contract assignment, I could only laugh at the callous behavior and the desire to purposely ignore me, especially since my contract was about to end and I was about to leave the organization very soon.

In the final moments of my contract, a meeting was held with the extended team including the program sponsor. During this meeting, the sponsor yelled at a senior employee and instructed the same individual to basically shut-up and not to say another word. I thought, "What?! This kind of behavior is allowed in a professional environment?!"

After the meeting, I consulted with the person who was insulted, demeaned, and not treated professionally to provide sympathy and support.

By this point, I was exhausted from my continuous battles with the program sponsor, the lack of management support to resolve the ongoing issues, the blatant disregard for professional decorum, and basic human respect. This was the first time in my career that I observed and was tired of watching someone acting as a bully, along with using the workplace as a personal playground.

During this program, I received months of verbal abuse and undue influence, even during the time it was widely known that I was personally sick, and my mom was hospitalized. Then, added to this the embarrassment, rudeness, and lack of civility to another individual, I decided that I wouldn't allow this uncivilized behavior to go unreported and unchallenged without providing formal documentation about this incident.

At this point, I decided to become a whistle-blower[8].

After months of unnecessary harassment and unrelenting questionable behavior, I decided to document the bullying behavior

---

[8] Whistle-blower – someone who provides information about another's wrongdoing

Merriam-Webster. Online. (merriam-webster.com/thesaurus/whistle-blower), retrieved: 4/5/13.

in an e-mail to the management and program team so that these issues were recorded.

The most significant reason that I documented the bullying behavior via e-mail was to document this behavior with a written record. This minimized the possibility that the management team could continue to ignore the actions and behaviors that the extended team was already aware.

Unfortunately, the organization's leaders never contacted me about any of the issues that were documented in my e-mail, which conveyed a lot about the inner workings of the management team and the organization.

Postlude

Years after this workplace bullying incident, I was at an event unrelated to any work activities. During this event, there was an insignificant disagreement with a family member of an employee who worked at this company about something that happened at the current, unrelated event.

Then, unexpectedly and without warning, the same uninvolved individual communicated hurtful, misleading information about me, and the incident detailed in this chapter. This communication extended the workplace bullying incident from several years earlier to a non-related current event.

The incredulous part about this unfortunate encounter was that uninformed information about the bullying incidents was communicated in a crowd to individuals who didn't have any reason to obtain the information.

This incident is even more shocking because the comment was made by someone who wasn't even directly or indirectly involved in the original incident.

Questions

1) What would you do if a colleague yelled at you loudly, verbally insulted, and disrespected you in front of your peers in a professional environment?

2) Is it ever appropriate for someone to yell at you at work? Why or why not?

3) What would you do if (while you spoke) someone talked over you and turned their back on you in an intentional effort to be rude?

4) If a colleague was yelled at during a public meeting, what would you do? Would you intervene? Would the incident be reported? Why or why not?

5) If you observed a colleague being abused, would you get involved? Why or why not?

6) If you decided to get involved, what action(s) would you take?

Lessons Learned

Bad behavior is bad behavior. At a certain point, bad behavior reaches a level that can no longer be condoned or ignored. Therefore, each of us has a responsibility to report any inappropriate behavior, especially bullying.

Involvement doesn't mean that you must become directly involved, but it does mean that action should be taken to document and/or report the issue (anonymously) so that others can resolve it.

If action isn't taken to prevent unnecessary and unwanted abuse, then the individuals who witness it and don't take action to prevent it are culpable. Moreover, the lack of inaction provides tacit approval of the actions and/or behaviors.

Bullying behavior should not be tolerated as there isn't any justification for watching abusive behavior and not acting, especially if the bullying behavior reaches a point that individual dignity and self-respect are compromised.

Taking action to provide information to others who have the authority and power to ensure that the bullying behavior no longer continues is much better than choosing to not get involved (while at the same time allowing someone to unnecessarily be or remain a bullying target).

Bullying Behavior Types:
- Aggressive
- Connectional
- Demeaning
- Extender
- Embarrassing
- Intimidating
- Positional

Chapter 37:

It's Not All About You

While preparing to leave a very demanding but rewarding consulting assignment, I eagerly sought my next career opportunity. During my job search, I was presented with an opportunity to work on my first government assignment.

After a few days on this assignment, I realized that the pace of the assignment was very slow. I was accustomed to working on assignments that were so busy that there was never an opportunity to get bored, which I really enjoyed.

While experiencing some downtime, I took a break to speak to a new colleague. During the conversation, I asked, "Is it always this slow?" The response, "You'll get used to it.", was unexpected. This comment would foreshadow things to come.

I stared at my computer screen most of the day because my government manager didn't provide any directions, which was troublesome to me. Therefore, I scheduled a meeting with my manager to ask for a more demanding and challenging assignment.

During the meeting with my manager, some direction was provided some direction; however, the direction was so generalized that it was nearly impossible for me to move forward without additional details and guidance.

After some consistent pressure from me to receive an actual assignment, my manager started to introduce me to some of the organization's directors. My belief was that these introductions would lead to some actual work, but I was mistaken.

On past assignments, there were not any issues with me demonstrating initiative to make progress, but, in this environment, it wasn't wanted or appreciated.

Regardless, I decided that I would take the initiative to contact some of the government resources to attempt to make some progress.

However, my efforts were not taken seriously as a contractor.

This lack of being taken seriously wasn't related to my ability, but my observation was that if my manager wasn't with me then the effort wasn't taken seriously. Therefore, I asked my manager (again) to assist me with the key stakeholders so that my work could be completed without exception.

The other issue I experienced on this assignment was the divisive environment.

Each contracting company was focused on maintaining its current task order, while also trying to obtain additional revenue generating opportunities. This competitive and cutthroat environment led to information hoarding and contractors not being overly helpful with each other.

This kind of infighting was foreign to me.

On my previous assignment, my team was almost entirely contractors. Nevertheless, I ensured that all resources were treated fairly and that the focus was on the achievement of the program objectives regardless of the contracting company.

After a few weeks, I realized that this environment wouldn't get any better. My observation was that my manager was more interested in building an empire based on the number of workers than the achievement of quantifiable results.

I wasn't adding any value to the organization, but not from a lack of trying. This lack of productivity was infuriating to me, as I was paid an extremely high salary to not be productive.

Sometimes an individual can receive a great salary, an optimal location, and an opportunity that could lead to a desirable job, but there is still something missing. Also, I didn't believe that this environment would get any better. Furthermore, I was wasting taxpayer money… including mine. Therefore, I decided to resign.

My contracting company was upset that I resigned because this was a key position, which the company needed to obtain additional positions within the organization. My contracting company's focus wasn't about me not doing any work; instead, the focus was all about the loss of revenue and a billable position.

After a discussion with my contracting company, I reluctantly decided to remain on the contract a little longer to give the company an opportunity to maintain its position within the organization.

My decision to stay was against my original reason to leave. A short time later, my decision to remain on the contract longer would be regretted.

After giving my manager and the environment an opportunity to change, I decided that I would no longer remain in a job that wasn't productive, lacked direction, unnecessarily wasted taxpayer money, I didn't add value, and was a waste of time.

Just prior to my departure from this organization, I identified and was hired for another position in the same organization. My new position reported to a different manager. I was excited by my new position, because it was extremely challenging. Also, this position would allow me to immediately add value to the organization.

My former manager wasn't happy that I quit and started to work for another manager in the same organization. My former manager might have felt embarrassed by my decision. This might be the reason that my former manager exerted considerable effort to ensure that I wouldn't keep my new position.

A short time into my new position, my former manager was on a mission against me.

My new manager confirmed to me that my former manager wasn't happy that I was still in the organization after resigning. At this point, I asked my new manager if this would be an issue, and the answer received wasn't expected.

My new manager told me that this situation was unfortunate. Then, my new manager communicated that it took a long time to obtain this position. I took this as a not-so-subtle message that I wouldn't be supported in my desire to maintain my new position.

My new manager wasn't interested in doing anything that might jeopardize this long sought-after management position. Therefore, we (my new manager and I) mutually decided that it wasn't possible for me to remain in my new position for completely different reasons.

I was very disappointed by this entire experience; however, this outcome was indicative of this government environment.

I used the rest of the day to complete my assignment; then, I left this contracting position for my next adventure.

A short time after I left this assignment, I ran into a director from a contracting company that worked for my original manager. This director made a snide comment to me, in a public grocery store, about my departure. The director made the comment loud enough so that others would hear the conversation trying to unnecessarily embarrass me.

This encounter reinforced my original decision to leave this toxic environment and not waste precious government resources.

Questions

1) What would you do if your job lacked direction, and you sat at your desk for almost the entire day without any work to do?

2) Would you stay at your job if there wasn't any work assigned? Why or why not?

3) What steps can be taken to help a manager who does not understand ways to create a vision to set direction?

4) What would you do if a manager retaliated against you after you no longer worked for the manager? Who could be contacted for assistance?

5) Were the reasons the jobs were left appropriate? Why or why not?

6) Do you agree with the decision to resign prior to obtaining the next position? Why or why not?

Lessons Learned

Doing the right thing is sometimes a challenge. However, doing the right thing is always the correct action.

Sometimes people won't like the decisions someone makes due to the impact on them or in trying to save face. However, it's not always possible to prevent someone from doing something to hurt you, but you always have control over the response to things done to you.

Employees can sometimes be placed into a situational conflict between competing positions:

- From the contracting company's perspective, the right thing to do was to generate billable time and identify opportunities to create additional revenue.

- From the original government manager's perspective, the goal was to build an empire, which wasn't in the best interest of the government.

- From the new manager's perspective, the goal was to maintain a long sought after job and not create any conflict that might jeopardize this position.

- From my perspective, my goal was to do the right thing and not be compensated for not doing any work.

It's everyone's responsibility to ensure that work, actions, and statements are honest. Moreover, work completed should add value; if not, changes should be made to become productive.

The collection of payments for the sake of earning income may be a method of getting rich, but the best riches come from being a good individual, operating in an ethical manner, and being true to an individual's character.

Doing the right thing can be challenging, but looking back on doing the wrong thing can have a heavy toll on someone's soul. Furthermore, there might not always be a chance to take correctable action(s) in the future.

Therefore, individuals should err on the side of caution and do the right thing instead of regretting doing something wrong.

Bullying Behavior Types:
- Aggressive
- Coercive
- Condescending
- Connectional
- Intimidating
- Knowledge
- Manipulative
- Positional

Chapter 38:

Accidents Happen

A colleague, my manager, and I met for an impromptu meeting in a small conference room.

During the meeting, my manager "passed gas." My manager didn't acknowledge the accident and continued the discussion.

A short time later my colleague stopped the meeting and asked, "What was that?"

The noise of "passed gas" was so loud that it was impossible for anyone to not recognize the sound and the source. My manager and I ignored the sound, and my colleague should have done the same.

After the question was asked, my manager was forced to acknowledge the "passed gas" before the meeting could continue.

Questions

1) Was it appropriate for the individual to ask, "What was that?" in reference to the "passed gas?" Why or why not?

2) What would you do if someone "passed gas" in a meeting?

3) Should anything be said to the individual who asked the question about the "passed gas" after the meeting? Why or why not?

Lessons Learned

Every incident that occurs isn't worth bringing to someone's attention, as there are many opportunities for each of us to have an embarrassing moment that we hope nobody notices or mentions.

Furthermore, intentionally trying to embarrass someone due to a bodily discharge is unprofessional and simply childish, as this incident could and should have been ignored.

Time and attention should be focused on things that matter, such as positive progress (instead of the use of someone's momentary unfortunate situation to embarrass).

Bullying Behavior Types:
- Demeaning
- Embarrassing

Chapter 39:

You're Not Worthy

This position involved reporting to two managers: a direct and a matrix manager.

A few weeks after I started this position, my manager and I reviewed an executive presentation. After the presentation was reviewed, my manager wanted a slide removed. Shortly thereafter, the presentation was reviewed with my matrix manager.

During the discussion with my matrix manager, I was told to keep the slide (the slide that my manager told me to remove) in the presentation. I informed my matrix manager that my manager wanted the slide taken out of the presentation. Then, the matrix manager said, "As long as we (the matrix manager and I) agreed, the slide would remain in the presentation."

This behavior was very questionable since my matrix manager was told that my manager wanted the slide removed.

After the meeting, I informed my manager about the direction received from my matrix manager. My manager didn't protest the inclusion of the slide; therefore, the slide remained in the presentation.

The next incident occurred shortly thereafter and was notable.

This incident was related to a desire to ratify a contract by a certain date. The only driver for this date was that my matrix manager communicated an arbitrary date to the executive team. However, my manager didn't indicate or communicate to me that this date was critical. Furthermore, the date provided by my matrix manager didn't impact the project implementation date or the project schedule.

After I assumed the leadership position for the contract negotiations from my matrix manager, there was increased concern by me that the contract wouldn't be signed by the date my matrix manager communicated to the executive team.

This concern about the contract execution was due to the extended team (whose feedback was essential) would be at an offsite meeting the following week.

Nevertheless, I worked diligently to ratify the contract by the matrix manager's communicated date despite the loss of a few working days due to the offsite meeting.

As the contract execution deadline approached, there were many contractual issues that couldn't be agreed upon. However, the vendor accepted my proposed corrections, even though some of the changes weren't in the vendor's best interest. If the vendor didn't provide blanket approval for the requested changes, then the contract negotiations might have continued for another month.

Regardless, the contract was executed. This milestone should have been a moment to celebrate; unfortunately, the celebration was deflated because my matrix manager took credit for the contact's successful execution by the communicated date.

The matrix manager's taking credit for the contract execution took a little away from the celebration for me, but there wasn't any time to dwell on this matter as the project was officially ready to begin.

The next major incident was related to an operational recommendation that was made by me after a project meeting.

During the meeting that the recommendation was developed, I identified that the organization wasn't ready to support the project given its current structure and the vendor's proposed solution. Therefore, I proactively assembled a team of key stakeholders (who also attended this meeting) to review the proposed solution and make a recommendation to the executive team about ways to address the impending issues.

My manager supported the team's proposal; however, first thing the next morning, just prior to the start of the project meeting, I was led to my matrix manager's office. Then, without hesitation or warning, I was informed by my matrix manager (in no uncertain terms) that recommendations (although vetted with the key stakeholders) were not allowed without the matrix manager's express approval.

> Note: My manager allowed me to work independently without having to seek advance approval, as my manager praised my initiative.

The meeting with my matrix manager was a little contentious; although, the discussion remained mostly professional. After this discussion, the matrix manager and I returned to the project meeting.

After the project meeting, I informed my manager about the discussion with my matrix manager. My manager then asked to be kept informed about any further incidents.

Later that week, as I prepared for the closeout of the kick-off meeting at my desk, my manager stopped by and said, "I cannot attend the closeout meeting due to a meeting conflict."

After a momentary pause, I asked my manager to attend the meeting, as I believed that the matrix manager would attempt to subvert and counter anything I said during the meeting.

During the kick-off closeout meeting as the project lead, I started to review the week's activities and action items. However, it didn't take long for my matrix manager to start to counter or discount almost every comment I offered to the team. Fortunately, my manager was present (by request due to my increased working challenges with my matrix manager), and was able to defend my positions, as needed.

A short time after the closeout meeting, I met with my matrix manager to discuss project updates. During this informal meeting, I used standard project management terminology. After using a term, the matrix manager corrected me on my terminology.

At this point, I began to explain the reason that the term was used. Then, before I could finish, my matrix manager asked me in a very nasty and harsh manner, "What do you know about product development?"

After being insulted, I began to explain that I had years of product development experience. Before I could complete my defense, my manager entered the matrix manager's office to ask an unrelated question.

My manager's interruption of the discussion was used by me as an opportunity to quickly exit this condescending conversation, which I was demeaned and insulted.

Later, my manager and I discussed the unprofessional and negative commentary I experienced with my matrix manager. These conversations with my manager became more frequent in the coming days.

A short time after this incident, the relationship between my matrix manager and I was about to go from bad to worse.

During a periodic meeting with my matrix manager, I was instructed to setup a meeting to discuss a project issue. I scheduled the meeting as instructed after I checked my matrix manager's schedule, along with the other required attendees.

Shortly after I sent the meeting invite, I received an e-mail from my matrix manager that chastised me about scheduling a meeting without checking the matrix manager's availability first.

I replied to my matrix manager's accusatory e-mail and communicated that the meeting was scheduled (based on my matrix manager's request) after I checked my matrix manager's schedule first for availability.

A short while later I received an e-mail from my matrix manager that informed me that the wrong e-mail was replied to in error, which I considered this e-mail very suspect.

On another occasion, my matrix manager accused me of being unethical because the nature of a private conversation with a vendor's project manager wasn't disclosed upon request by my matrix manager. The details of my private conversation were not disclosed to my matrix manager because the conversation wasn't related to work (and the fact that it was a "private" conversation).

It was highly questionable to be accused of being unethical without any justification.

As the relationship with my matrix manager continued to deteriorate, I noticed that a pregnant colleague appeared to be in distress. This was especially of concern as she was close to her delivery date. After I verified that she was doing better, I returned to my desk.

After I returned to my desk, I overheard other coworkers starting to check on my pregnant colleague; at this point, I returned to her desk and offered to contact my doctor who was located nearby.

As I attempted to provide information about my doctor's location, my matrix manager gave me a dismissive look (as to convey that this is none of your business) and escorted the pregnant colleague away from me into the matrix manager's office.

My concerns about the matrix manager's behavior continued to grow daily; therefore, I spoke to my manager about scheduling a meeting between the three of us.

My manager didn't appear to want to get involved, so I scheduled a meeting with my matrix manager alone to discuss our increasingly strained and difficult relationship.

The goal of this meeting with my matrix manager was to identify the source of our conflict, review roles and responsibilities, and identify a plan to move forward.

Roles and responsibilities were reviewed during this meeting to determine if our relationship challenges were related to overlapping project responsibilities.

Unfortunately, my reconciliation plans quickly dissipated as the meeting was very icy.

At times, during our meeting, my matrix manager directed long stares at me as if there was an attempt to intimidate me. This occurred while I tried to discover the reason(s) for the harassment and hostility toward me. Unfortunately, this meeting didn't get us any closer to resolution about the reason(s) for our more than strained relationship.

During my next biweekly meeting with my manager, I expressed concerns that my relationship with my matrix manager had rapidly deteriorated beyond repair. At this point, I told my manager that I felt that my matrix manager didn't like me, and there wasn't anything that I could do to repair the relationship.

The next week I decided to send an e-mail to the executive team to provide a preview of the software, as it began to obtain structure.

From my past software development and management experiences, development information was shared with stakeholders early, often, and throughout the development process. Normally, this type of sharing prevented later surprises and allowed the team to course correct early in the development process if there were any issues.

I was mindful of my matrix manager's almost continuous attacks to almost anything I did for the project. For this reason, I read my e-mails several times before sending to ensure that any e-mails wouldn't receive any backlash, as other e-mails I sent resulted in me being admonished by my matrix manager.

I performed these extra reviews to insulate myself from the increasing number of attacks, which at times were very personal.

Some of the executive team members responded that the initial development didn't meet expectations for various reasons. The responses received from the executive team were not a surprise since their input wasn't solicited while the software requirements or the software itself was developed.

While meeting with my matrix manager about an unrelated issue, my matrix manager asked me as if I were a child, "What were you thinking when you sent that e-mail?"

At this point, I explained my rationale for providing the executive team with a development preview; however, my matrix manager didn't want to listen and was clearly not happy with my decision to send the development preview e-mail.

It is important to note that (as the project lead) there wasn't any communication or direction from my manager that prevented me from providing updates to the project team and/or the executive team.

Another item of concern that was discussed with my matrix manager was about the manner in which a character was used in the software development. My concern was related to the negative use of a female and a minority as the underperformer in the software development, as women and minorities are often portrayed in a negative light. This concern was also shared with the key development managers.

After my concerns were communicated to my matrix manager and the development managers, I asked for consideration that a nonminority character be used as the underperformer.

A response to my request for reconsideration of the use of a minority and a female character in a negative way was never received by anyone involved with the project.

During another meeting with my matrix manager, after my request was sent to not use a character in the software development, my matrix manager told me that a peer of the matrix manager would send an e-mail the next day. My matrix manager advised that the email would be in reference to concerns about the project and the state of development (as seen by the software preview).

The next day (true to my matrix manager's words) an e-mail was received from a peer manager that included wording very close to the comments foretold by my matrix manager a day earlier.

This e-mail also included comments that my matrix manager and their team worked very hard on the development. The e-mail (I believe intentionally) excluded any references to the extended team's or my efforts. Moreover, this e-mail appeared to purposely discount any of my contributions as the project lead.

As a follow-up to the meeting with my matrix manager, my manager and I agreed that it was beneficial that the executive team's concerns were identified early in the development process. This identification allowed the issues to be fixed prior to the completion of major development.

My matrix manager continued to express discontent with almost every action, decision, or any question that originated from me.

After the ongoing battles with my matrix manager and the lack of acknowledgement about minority and racial sensitivity, I questioned whether this was the right environment for me. I felt that an employee shouldn't need to be in a constant battle about the job, with territorial challenges, and especially with any manager.

A few days later I decided to resign for my mental peace of mind. The reason I resigned was that I refused to allow anyone to treat me with less dignity and respect than I not only deserved, but also required.

It was a bittersweet departure, as my manager and I were great partners. It was nice to be able to collaborate with a manager who was concerned about the work and not a perception of self-importance.

On my last day, my manager and I met with a human resources manager to complete the exit interview. I went to the exit interview with all my personal possessions and my company issued equipment with me.

The human resources manager greeted us and laughed while saying, "No one has ever come to an exit interview with their bags packed,"

The fact that my possessions were already with me during the exit interview was a sign that I wanted to leave the building as quickly as possible. Nevertheless, I emphasized my blistering desire to leave this job to the human resource manager.

My disclosures to the human resources manager (about my challenges with my matrix manager) should have been used as an indication and an invitation for the human resources manager to inquire about the reasons that I wanted to make a hasty departure. However, this didn't occur.

Even though I didn't volunteer to disclose my detailed concerns about my challenges with my matrix manager due to being exhausted by the ongoing confrontations, the human resources manager missed an opportunity to determine the source of my necessity to hastily leave the company.

Regardless, during the exit interview with my manager present (without any objection from me), I very briefly conveyed to the human resources manager the ongoing, almost constant attacks from my matrix manager that made it impossible for me to remain at the company.

Then, I expressed my disappointment about not being able to continue to work for the company and with my manager.

After the exit interview, my manager and I walked into the hallway. At this point, my manager and I gave each other a hug; I thanked my manager for the opportunity, and then I left the building with my dignity and self-respect still intact.

Questions

1) What would you do if a manager you worked with and for indirectly constantly harassed you?

2) Would you inform anyone about the harassment? Why or why not?

3) Does a manager have a responsibility to protect an employee from harassment? Why or why not?

4) Does any manager have the right to speak to an employee in a disrespectful manner? If so, when might it be appropriate? If not, why not?

5) Would you inform management about an issue that on the surface may be okay, but affected you personally? Why or why not?

6) What obligation(s) does management have to address any personal issues identified by an employee?

7) Were you ever in a situation that your personal beliefs conflicted with your assignment? If so, what happened? If not, what would you do?

8) How much harassment would be required for you to quit a job? Would other factors impact your ability to endure the harassment? If so, what are these factors?

9) Are there any reasons that you would quit a job without another job already? Why or why not?

Lessons Learned

An individual's objectives for the use of bullying behavior are seldom clear, but the impact of the bullying behavior is always felt.

Bullying behavior is a lot more difficult to address if the bully is a senior leader. An individual's level in the organization may make an issue harder to address due to the power that the senior leader holds over someone's position. Regardless of positional power, nobody has the right or authority to bully resources.

Once the bullying behavior is identified, an employee should begin to keep a log of the incidents, including dates, times, and severity of the incidents.

A trusted advisor (inside or outside of the company) should be contacted to seek advice. Also, human resources should be contacted and involved with any potential harassment issue(s), as human resources is responsible for policy guidance and enforcement.

As for behavior that may be against an individual's moral beliefs, it is more than appropriate to identify the source of any issue(s) and address them. Many times, an issue can be addressed by discussing the matter with the offending party.

If this approach does not work or isn't appropriate, then a manager or a human resources representative can be engaged to aid with issue resolution.

Resources (e.g., employees, consultants) should not have to deal with any type of bullying behavior; however, if bullying behavior does occur, it is an employee's responsibility to ensure that management, human resources, and if appropriate outside parties are notified to protect yourself and others from unwanted abuse.

Bullying Behavior Types:
- Aggressive
- Coercive
- Condescending
- Connectional
- Demeaning
- Extender
- Fear
- Intimidating
- Manipulative
- Positional

Chapter 40:

Company Responsibility

Companies have a responsibility to ensure that the workplace is safe from harassment, including any unwanted physical contact. Resources (e.g., employees, consultants) shouldn't be threatened in an environment in which much of their life is spent.

All management levels (especially executive management) must set an example and standard for all resources to follow.

Companies should do the following to minimize workplace bullying:

- Demonstrate respect and fair treatment for all resources

- Create behavioral policies and standards related to appropriate conduct

- Enforce any policies and/or standards timely, fairly, and without retaliation

- Discuss behavioral expectations within each manager's team at least twice a year

- Review policies and standards annually to determine if updates are required

Companies should provide periodic interpersonal skills training, which will allow resources an opportunity to obtain reinforcement about reasonable and acceptable workplace behavior. Furthermore, interpersonal training can assist teams to improve self-awareness, issue management, relationship management, and communication skills.

Companies that do not maintain environments for resources to be respected and protected can expect inappropriate behavior that leads to abuse, reduced productivity, retaliation, conflict, absenteeism, or other negative consequences.

<u>Note:</u> Special consideration should be given to consultants who in theory should be protected under a company's policies. However, in practice, consultants may be more unlikely to report bullying behavior due to the non-permanency of the employment relationship.

Also, the human resource policies for a company will most likely not be as well known to a consultant. Therefore, consultants may believe that a company's human resource policies don't apply or won't protect them.

Chapter 41:

Individual Responsibility

Individuals have a responsibility to protect themselves from workplace bullying regardless of time, place, frequency, or severity.

Often, bullies will use their tactics during periods in which others aren't there to witness the harassment, but this isn't always the case.

This is a reason that bullying behavior should always be dealt with and/or reported as quickly as possible to minimize the possibility and opportunity for recurrence.

Individuals should take the following steps to deal with workplace bullying:

- Become familiar with the types of bullying behavior (described in Chapter 2)

- Review company policies and/or standards to understand the way bullying (may be listed under harassment) is addressed

- Communicate to the bully that the behavior isn't acceptable, won't be tolerated, and will be reported

    o Do not engage the bully directly if there is a fear of a physical attack

- Keep a record of any bullying incident(s) with a copy in an offsite location, which includes the date, time, and a description of any incident(s)

- Report any incident to a member of the management team and/or the human resources department to create a formal record

    o This action will allow the procedure to be monitored, reviewed, and updated (as necessary)

Bullying incidents that are not reported can lead to incidents that continue, get worse, and/or impact others. Furthermore, bullying incidents cannot be properly addressed unless the incidents are reported, documented, and/or prevented in a timely manner.

> Note: The Equal Employment Opportunity Commission (EEOC – eeoc.gov) provides information about hostile work environments

Chapter 42:

Bullies Impact on

Their Targets

Workplace bullying can have many impacts on resources and to companies if not properly addressed.

Many times, the issues associated with workplace bullying are not known and/or fully understood primarily due to workplace bullying incidents either not being reported or being underreported.

Potential issues created by workplace bullying:

- Absenteeism - lack of work attendance

- Death – the loss of life due to stress related to bullying behavior

- Employee Dissatisfaction – the job and/or the job environment isn't liked

- Insomnia – loss of sleep

- Lost Employee – a resource who leaves a job for another opportunity

- Impact on Morale – negative impact on an individual's attitude about the work environment and sometimes life

- Mental Well-Being – someone's personal happiness and/or mental attitude is impacted

- Productivity/Efficiency - work isn't completed as quickly or as well as it could be performed

- Self-worth – an impact to feelings of personal value

- Stress - feeling pressure about the work environment

- Suicide – the taking of an individual's life due to no longer being able to deal with bullying

- <u>Transference</u> - impact to life areas away from work

- <u>Weight Loss/Gain</u> - change in physical appearance

This is a partial list of issues that bullies can impose on their targets.

It's very important that bullying targets report any bullying behavior or unwanted attention. Also, companies should have a zero-tolerance policy for any bullying behavior, along with having specific guidance on ways to address and prevent workplace bullying, including unwelcome sexual advances.

Chapter 43:

Workplace Bullying Statistics

According to the Society of Human Resource Management's (SHRM) "SHRM Survey Findings: Workplace Bullying (2/28/12)"[9]:

- 51% of organizations surveyed experienced incidents of workplace bullying

- 44% of organizations surveyed do not have workplace bullying policies

- 22% of organizations surveyed do not have a grievance process to investigate bullying allegations

- 57% of organizations surveyed do not conduct regular bullying prevention/awareness training

Information about the SHRM's methodology used for the workplace bullying survey:

- Survey was conducted May 9 – 27, 2011

- Random sample of 401 Human Resources (HR) professionals from SHRM membership

- 15% response rate with a margin of error +/- 5%

---

[9] Society for Human Resource Management (SHRM). "SHRM Survey Findings: Workplace Bullying" (2/28/12). Online (http://shrm.org/research/surveyfindings/articles/pages/workplacebullying.aspx), Retrieved: 3/12/13

Chapter 44:
Underreporting
Workplace Bullying

The number of workplace bullying incidents is most likely a lot higher than the number reported incidents. The most probable reason for lower reported incidents of workplace bullying is that bullying targets do not want to report the workplace incidents for various reasons.

Resources (e.g., employee, consultants) may not report a workplace bullying incident due to:

- Fear – expectation that something bad will happen if an incident is reported

- Job Loss – loss of a job due to an incident report

- Perception – belief that nothing will change if an incident is reported or that others will think negatively about an individual who reports an incident

- Process – the process to report an incident and/or protect a target after an incident isn't understood

- Retaliation – backlash received by an individual who reports an incident

- Lack of Clarity About Rights – incorrect belief that an incident is based on a management style; therefore, the resource must deal with the behavior or leave the organization and/or company

It's important that companies remove or eliminate any potential barriers for reporting workplace bullying incidents to ensure safe, productive, and friendly work environments for all resources.

Chapter 45:

Ways to Help Bullies

Bullies may or may not realize that their behavior is considered bullying. However, it is a company's and a target's responsibility to ensure that any bullying behavior is addressed and/or reported as quickly as possible. Otherwise, a bullying incident is left unresolved and could lead to additional unwarranted and unwanted harassment.

<u>Bullies can be helped by:</u>

- <u>Counseling</u> – the use of professional resources with the bully to attempt to identify the source of the bullying behavior

- <u>Mentoring</u> – partner the bully with well-respected resources to assist the bully with completing tasks without bullying behavior

- <u>Training</u> – teach the bully about ways to accomplish work tasks without the use of bullying behavior

- <u>Terminating</u> – resources that cannot or are unwilling to change must be removed from the company

Bullying is a behavioral issue that must be addressed immediately. Otherwise, the negative impact of bullying behavior can lead to organizational challenges (e.g., reduced productivity, impact on morale, lost employees).

Chapter 46:
Parting Thoughts

The examples provided in this book are small selections of bullying incidents that were experienced during my career. The unfortunate part is that similar or worse incidents occur every day in offices around the world.

The challenge is that sometimes good or excellent job performance isn't enough to prevent incidents of workplace bullying, as bullying can be unrelated to actual job performance. Workplace bullying can be related to items such as race, sex, religion, appearance, intelligence, speaking ability, or other factors.

The first few factors (race, sex, and religion) are protected classes under Title VII of the Equal Employment Opportunity Act protected by the Equal Employment Opportunity Commission (EEOC). The other factors (appearance, intelligence, and speaking ability) are not protected classes; therefore, individuals can and do legally discriminate due to some of the craziest reasons.

For example, in 2011, John Stone (a car salesperson) was fired because he wore a Green Bay Packers tie to work. Mr. Stone was told numerous times to remove the tie and upon his multiple refusals to remove the Green Bay Packers tie Mr. Stone was terminated.[10]

Responsible companies will vigorously enforce policies that protect all resources (e.g., employees, consultants) from any type of discriminatory, harassing, questionable, or unwanted behavior.

Bullying is a serious issue and should be dealt with in an expeditious manner similar to the way other unethical behavior is addressed. Furthermore, companies should act swiftly and decisively to stop, eliminate, and prevent any workplace bullying actions and/or

---

[10] Neil, Martha. "Chicago Fan Wears Packers Tie to Work on Monday and is Fired." American Bar Association Journal (2011). Online (http://www.abajournal.com/news/article/chicago_fan_wears_packers_tie_to_w ork_on_monday_and_is_fired/), retrieved: 3/25/13.

behaviors.

Individuals must also be aware of their rights and should not let any discriminatory or harassing behavior go unchallenged or unreported.

Some types of bullying can be very aggressive and direct while other types of bullying can be very subtle so that it's not realized until later or until it happens too many times.

Nobody should have to deal with or tolerate harassment.

Identifying bullying behavior isn't as easy as using checklists, as there are a lot of different bullying types. The most important guide to identify incidents of workplace bullying is to rely on a reasonable perception of the bullying target or others that may witness a bullying incident.

There is sometimes a small distinction between bullying behavior, bad management, and/or bad manners. Therefore, it is very important for the perceived target to address any potential issue(s) as quickly as possible. This will allow any issue(s) created by the bully to be addressed and fixed without any unnecessary delay.

After reading this book, ask your human resources department for a copy of the company's anti-harassment policy to determine if workplace bullying is included in the protections listed. If not, ask your human resources department to update the policy to not only protect you, but also to protect other resources and the company.

As a bullying target, the time that you do not want to determine if a policy exists or seek protection under it is while under attack.

If you or someone you know is bullied, then it's your responsibility to get involved in the matter. Addressing inappropriate behavior doesn't mean that you must personally get involved. Involvement could just involve ensuring that someone with the power to stop bullying behavior is aware of an issue, even if it means reporting the knowledge anonymously.

If all of us are not vigilant in the prevention of any type of bullying, we all lose, and the next bullying target could be you. Therefore, let's collectively work to take the power away from the bullies and return the power to the bullying targets.

This book documents many of my very personal experiences with workplace bullies.

The bullies I encountered at work are not much different than the bullies who operate at schools. The main difference is the environment; therefore, let's protect all our environments (regardless of location) from unnecessary and preventable abuse, harassment, and rights infringement.

It's time for all of us (e.g., individuals, corporations, governments) to take decisive action to change the societal rules, policies, and laws to protect workplace bullying targets. Immediate change will ensure that all workers aren't unnecessarily abused while trying to raise a family, build a career, or pursue personal happiness.

Everyday individuals reluctantly choose to remain in abusive environments due to systematic failures that allow bullies to dominant, abuse, demean, mistreat, and cause individuals to leave jobs because there are not any available, documented, or enforced protection remedies.

It is our collective responsibility to prevent workplace bullying and protect workplace bullying targets.

Life is too short to allow yourself or others to be put into or remain in a position that makes anyone miserable.

So, from now on, don't accept unnecessary workplace abuse; label the harassment by its rightful name... bullying.

Remember, *"Bullies...They're in Your Office, Too."*

So, after reading this book, are you one?!

> Note: To learn more about this topic, watch Dr. Young's presentation "Workplace Bullying – It's More Than Hurt Feelings" (youtu.be/nveyUirn_Dk).

References

Harvard Business Review. "How Bullying Manifests at Work – and How to Stop It" (11/4/22). Online (hbr.org/2022/11/how-bullying-manifests-at-work-and-how-to-stop-it), Retrieved: 10/2/23

Healthy Workplace Bill. Online. (healthyworkplacebill.org), retrieved: 10/2/23

Merriam-Webster. Online. (merriam-webster.com/thesaurus/whistle-blower), retrieved: 4/5/13.

Neil, Martha. "Chicago Fan Wears Packers Tie to Work on Monday and is Fired." American Bar Association Journal (2011). Online (abajournal.com/news/article/chicago_fan_wears_packers_tie_to_work_on_monday_and_is_fired/), retrieved: 3/25/13.

Society for Human Resource Management (SHRM). "SHRM Survey Findings: Workplace Bullying" (2/28/12). Online (shrm.org/research/surveyfindings/articles/pages/workplacebullying.aspx), Retrieved: 3/12/13.

The Health Workplace Campaign. "PA becomes the 25th State – 10th in 2013." (3/25/13). Online (healthyworkplacebill.org/blog/maine-24), Retrieved: 5/29/13.

About the Author

Dr. S. L. Young is an author, professor, career coach, former HuffPost contributor, founder of the educational non-profit organization "Saving Our Communities at Risk Through Educational Services (SOCARTES – socartes.org)," founder of the for-profit company "Beyond SPRH, LLC – beyondsprh.com)," and former host of "Beyond Just Talk with S. L. Young." The topics of his books include belief, communication, negotiation, time management, workplace bullying, ethics, overcoming challenges, and inspirational quotes.

In 2012, Dr. Young became an author with the release of his first book in the "It's a Crazy World… Learn From It" series.

Dr. Young graduated from the American University in Washington, D.C. with a Bachelor of Science in Business Administration (BSBA) degree in International Business with a marketing concentration. He also graduated from The George Washington University in Washington, D.C. with two degrees: Master of Business Administration (MBA) in Finance and Investments with a human resources concentration and a Master of Science (M.S.) in Project Management. In 2023, at Marymount University, he successfully defended his Doctorate (Ed.D.) in Educational Leadership and Organizational Innovation. The focus of his doctoral research was "Student Engagement's Impact on Academic Performance for Nontraditional Students in a Community College Environment."

In 2022, Dr. Young was inducted into and became a life member of The Honor Society of Phi Kappa Phi. In 2023, he was inducted into The Honor Society of Kappa Delta Pi. Additionally, he's a life-member of the professional business fraternity of Alpha Kappa Psi.

Dr. Young's professional career includes approximately fifteen years with Fortune 500 companies, including Bell Atlantic, MCI, Sprint Nextel, and various consulting engagements, in the areas of billing, customer service, engineering, finance, information technology, network security, operations, product development, and software quality assurance.

Dr. Young, for nearly fifteen years, has taught a variety of classes (i.e., Introduction to Business, Entrepreneurship, Business Communication, Marketing, Small Business Management, Organizational Behavior, and Principles of Management at the Northern Virginia Community College. He has also taught at Marymount University for over three years.

In 2012, Dr. Young created SOCARTES to share life and business lessons with individuals in opportunity "at-risk" communities. Through his work with this organization, he created additional pathways for him to give-back to and make meaningful connections in various communities.

Dr. Young's passion to help others is fueled based on his abilities to excel academically and professionally. These accomplishments occurred after being directed to leave high school in tenth grade, graduating in the bottom 8% of his high school class, and leaving several colleges prior to becoming actively engaged in the process of learning. These experiences drove his desires to tirelessly help others in meaningful ways and various environments.

In January 2015, Dr. Young launched Beyond SPRH, which provides solution-oriented services to help individuals and organizations to maximize output potential.

In 2018, Dr. Young received special recognition for his work to educate an incarcerated population. The first was the Martin Luther King, Jr. Drum Major Innovative Service Award from the U.S. Department of Education for Faith-Based and Neighborhood Partnerships, in collaboration with the White House Initiative for Educational Excellence for African-Americans. The second was the Distinguished County Service Award from Volunteer Arlington (a program of the Leadership Center for Excellence).

Dr. Young is driven to share his knowledge that leads to developmental opportunities (especially for underserved and marginalized communities). Through his authentic lived-experiences overcoming challenges, Dr. Young works tirelessly to inspire others to overcome challenges and pursue their dreams, too.

Dr. Young's published works:

- Above Expectations – My Story: an unlikely journey from almost failing high school to becoming a college professor

- Bullies… They're In Your Office, Too: Could you be one?

- Choosing To Take A Stand: Changed me, my life, and my destiny

- Ethical Opportunity Cost: It's a matter of choice

- It's a Crazy World… Learn From It:

    o Part I – Taking Care of Me

    o Part II – Moving Forward

    o Part III – Keeping It Going

    o Part IV – The Journey Continues

- Management Spotlight:

    o Belief

    o Communication

    o Critical Thinking/Thick-Skin

    o Negotiation

    o Time Management

    o Workplace Bullying

- Soft Skills Development:

    o Belief

    o Communication

    o Critical Thinking/Thick-Skin

    o Negotiation

    o Time Management

- Turning Darkness Into Light: Inspiring lessons after a near-suicide

www.ingramcontent.com/pod-product-compliance
Lightning Source LLC
Chambersburg PA
CBHW071412170526
45165CB00001B/252